MICHAEL
JACKSON

THIS IS A CARLTON BOOK

First published in Great Britain in 2009.
This edition published in 2014 by Carlton Books Limited
20 Mortimer Street
London W1T 3JW

Copyright 2009, 2014 © Carlton Books Limited

A CIP catalogue for this book is available
from the British Library.

ISBN: 978-1-78097-545-0

Printed in Dubai

MICHAEL JACKSON

THE KING OF POP

CHRIS ROBERTS

CARLTON
BOOKS

CONTENTS

INTRODUCTION

"He is beautiful, feline, febrile. Michael Jackson at 39 is the child within; the child without reality's picket fence. This show is gross indulgence, narcissism, bombast. It is net magic, fantasy, travel, displacement, dissimulation, derailment. He dances with grace notes; his knees have Elvis dust. He adds to the sum of unusual and radiant things that have been attempted." I saw a Michael Jackson show at Wembley Stadium on July 26, 1997 and this is what I wrote. I went on, for some time. "He has a Messiah complex devouring every pore. He moves the temple of his body and the chimes of his ego sound in the breeze of our awe. He is on fire, is a panther in Astaire's weightless heaven. Then, that intergalactic smile. He wants us for his moonbeams. 'Stop pressuring me,' he chants, but he loves it."

At some point in this show he emerged from a pod-like rocket ship, convinced he was an astronaut made of gold. He stared down the crowd and silently milked the love, sometimes for ninety seconds or more. There were gangsters-and-molls set-pieces, a werewolf mask for "Thriller", the ceremonial donning of the glove for "Billie Jean". He dangled from a crane, suspended above our heads, for "Earth Song", "both acrobat and preacher". He pretended to cry between "I'll be..." and "...there", and it was more moving than when real people really cry. A tank burst through a wall onstage, and Michael stopped it. A little girl gave a soldier a flower and he laid down his gun.

"Mock if you will, but Michael Jackson is still big. If the genre got small, that's hardly his fault. The closing firework display seems puny without his presence. Jackson does not hug the shore. He knows the route to giddy rapture and for this can be forgiven anything. Onstage, he lives a stream of silky, seraphic lifetimes. That's entertainment."

It was only ever going to be this great transiently.

PREVIOUS PAGE: Shooting for the moon: Michael Jackson live in New York in 1997.

LEFT: With the Jackson 5 at the Mill Run Playhouse in 1974.

RIGHT: Jackson paints London's Wembley Stadium red.

That, too, is entertainment. He had been even better before. He wasn't going to get better now.

Youth was a dream from which the incomparable Michael Jackson found it painful and bewildering to wake up. "I'll always be Peter Pan in my heart," he once said. And that isn't always productive in the big bad world. The very Otherness which made him, in his best years, bigger and brighter than the rest, that set him apart as a superstar beyond peer, never down to earth, troubled him in later life. His death, on June 25, 2009, shocked the world, but may have healed his soul. The "greatest song and dance man of all time" had died before being the fading of youth grew any more unbearable.

That date will now forever be fixed in pop culture legend. Like the deaths of James Dean, Marilyn Monroe, Elvis Presley, John F. Kennedy, John Lennon and Princess Diana, it became an instant where-were-you-when-you-heard-the-news? moment. The falling of an icon displaced wars, famines and coups from television screens worldwide. Internet traffic – practically invented for such an occurrence – jammed with tears and tributes, gossip and guesswork. TMZ.com announced the news six minutes before Jackson had actually been confirmed dead. Google and Twitter buckled; Wikipedia couldn't handle the number of sudden edits and re-edits. The world jolted, rocked by a seismic supernova.

Everywhere, soon, you could hear the delicious romanticism of "Got To Be There" and "Ain't No Sunshine", the alchemy of the opening seconds of "Don't Stop 'Til You Get Enough", the matchless strut and finger-snap of "Billie Jean", the watershed riffing of "Beat It" and "Smooth Criminal", the whipcrack of "The Way You Make Me Feel", the falsetto gone-gone-gone whoops on the coda of "The Man In The Mirror", the sweetness of his voice on "Human Nature". Even the later ballads, laden with messianic pomp, seemed now possessed... of spirit, a cry for help, a plea to our better nature, something. Michael Jackson was young again, in full bloom, innocent.

Stunned crowds gathered in Hollywood, where he'd been living. In Harlem, New York, where the Apollo Theatre swiftly erected a memorial billboard. In Gary, Indiana, where Jackson was born and grew up. From Moscow to Beijing, London to Mexico, there were candlelight vigils and cathartic songs. There was even planet-wide denial as news stations correctly waited for absolute confirmation before declaring the reports of Michael's death to be true and not the results of scurrilous rumours. Gradually, after initial shell-shocked silence, the reactions of those who had known him filtered through. "Just as there will never be another Fred Astaire or Chuck Berry or Elvis Presley," said Steven Spielberg, "there will never be another Michael Jackson." Quincy Jones said, "I'm devastated. Divinity brought our souls together and allowed us to do what we could through the Eighties. That music is played in every corner of the world, and the reason is because he had it all – talent, grace and professionalism. I've lost my little brother today and part of my soul has gone with him." *Time* magazine published its first special issue since 9/11. The US Congress observed a moment of silence. "I will miss his light, his star, I will miss how he caused other people to become great because of his greatness," offered Donna Summer.

Said P. Diddy, "He made the music come to life. He made me believe in magic."

The plan had been for magic to return two weeks later, on July 13. Jackson of course was set to make what he and his fans had hoped would be one of the great showbiz comebacks, embarking on a 50-date residency at London's O2 Arena, before a total of almost a million spectators. Even announcing these shows – to be his first full live performances in 12 years – on March 5, he'd drawn 7,000 fans and 350 reporters. "This is it," he'd insisted. "These will be my final performances in London. When I say this is it, I really mean this will be it. This is the final curtain call."

The cruel irony is palpable. Tickets had sold in double figures per second. Michael had begun training, rehearsing, trying to get himself fit for duty. He wanted and needed to prove that the King of Pop was alive and well and hungry to reclaim his throne. That he still had the vocal chops – the arrow-tip yelps, the oceanic sighs – and the Futurist-painting moves. That he still had what Astaire had once described, witnessing the new contender, as "rage in his feet".

OPPOSITE: MJ – The man with the magic moves.

ABOVE: With close friend Elizabeth Taylor at the Shrine Auditorium in LA, January 1989.

OPPOSITE: A memorial to Michael at the BET Awards, July 2009.

As always, rumour and speculation abounded. Yet although many commentators were quick to claim they saw it coming, nobody had really anticipated what happened on June 25. Just hours after rehearsals for the imminent shows, an emergency call from his rented L.A. house. Paramedics rushing him to hospital. Attempts to resuscitate him. But no. His heart had failed. He was gone, at 50. The boy who'd never grown up now never would.

Yet with Michael Jackson's music and videos ubiquitous again, the world remembered the time. Remembered how his best records existed in a realm of their own, free of tethers and genres, free of the self-imposed constraints of more self-conscious mortals, high above the bustle and bluff of the everyday, the temporarily diverting. How his videos tore up the templates. How his influence shaped so much of popular culture, since. How he sound-tracked so many lives, across three generations, as a boy, as the King of Pop, and even as the increasingly bizarre enigma known as Wacko Jacko. How his voice could forget there were, supposedly, limits. How his young body shook up the rulebook. How it was. How it now stands a better chance of continuing to be, frozen in the spotlight of nostalgia.

The word "legend" is bandied around too liberally, but that's what we're dealing with here. This book celebrates the man-child who was the world's most popular entertainer. His arc is generally perceived as having had three main phases: the boy star, the man superstar, the boy-man hyperstar. We'll track through one of the most spectacular, provocative careers in history. What made his fans so loyal and devoted, through light and darkness? How did his charisma, talent and strangeness enchant across the world? Which of his albums – he sold hundreds of millions in life and that number is rising at speed now – were of their moment, and which are timeless? Did his eccentricities serve to boost his standing, or diminish it? Was he fundamentally too sensitive, too vulnerable, for the constant glare of attention and publicity which he couldn't help courting? To what extent did his later years tarnish the glow? Was Neverland a gilded cage? Did he only feel safe on stage for most of his life, then finally fear it? What was it like to be Michael Jackson?

"I get embarrassed easily," he once said. "I'm more comfortable on stage than any other place. It's the greatest place in the world. I just light up. It's magic. I'm here on Earth for a reason, and that's my job, to make me people happy. I've been doing it for so long." He added, "Being around everyday people, I feel strange. It's hard to live in the real world, in my position. I try to, sometimes, but people won't deal with me in that way, because they see me differently." He was just 22 when he said this.

He'd been on stage pretty much since he could walk, never mind moonwalk. Born August 29 in 1958, his father had him joining his brothers in performances by the age of five. It rapidly became evident that he was an all-singing all-dancing prodigy, so the die was cast. The Jackson 5 were Motown hit-makers by 1969. Michael was signed to the world's then best record label aged nine, and on the cover of *Rolling Stone* aged 11. With dazzling routines and some of the greatest singles in pop's lifetime, the Jackson brothers charmed the flares off the early Seventies.

Michael's ascension to solo star status was inevitable, but surely not many foresaw how far it would go. After 1979's *Off The Wall* set a ferociously high standard, the landmark works *Thriller* and then *Bad* went on to dominate the Eighties. The former (1982) remains the biggest

selling album of all time, with, at the latest count, an improbable 109 million copies sold worldwide. It has been preserved by the American Library of Congress as "culturally significant". "I am always writing a potpourri of music," he said. "I want to give the world escapism through the wonder of great music. And to reach the masses."

Bad (1987) is merely the third biggest commercial success ever. These albums spawned a stream of classic genre-bending hit singles which married funk, pop, soul and rock, and each of which merit eulogy. Such trademark tropes as the moonwalk, the red jacket and the one white glove became household terms. Jackson's videos, pushing the envelope until it folded in on itself, fuelled the rise of MTV. And as television embraced music and the medium and the message developed a new synergy, his live shows, gorging on visual flourishes and an atmosphere both carnal and neo-religious, prompted mass hysteria.

In the Nineties came complexity. His appearance changed, his skin colour changed, and he became ever more the subject of media scrutiny, a mysterious figure prone to reclusiveness and illness who constantly defied predictability. A shapeshifter. His records (such as *Dangerous* (1991), *HIStory* (1995) and *Invincible* (2001) still sold in huge quantities, though not as huge as before. Two marriages ensued – one, in a twist that only J. G. Ballard could have conceived – to Elvis Presley's daughter Lisa-Marie. He had three children, in unconventional circumstances. Everything Jackson did from this point seemed to provoke more scandal, which enormous services to charity couldn't dispel. His later years were marked by trauma, trials and financial minefields. Yet in one fell swoop that announcement of his return to the live arena, clarifying that in the eyes of his countless fans he was unassailable, seemed to offer the hope of a happier ending.

And then came the news. And the reactions to the reactions to the news. The tragedy is evident, and the media frenzy that will undoubtedly continue for years won't always be pretty. The redeeming beauty is that the unique Michael Jackson, whose masterpieces kicked and flew and whirled and levitated, will now remain forever a butterfly, a riddle, a myth, a mystery, a thing full of magic.

away and be just like them."

Joe was a strict father, hands on. Michael would years later tell Oprah Winfrey on TV, "There's a lot about my past life, my adolescence and my father that makes me very sad." He would learn about Joe's temper when he playfully put a spider on La Toya's bed. He would get used to it as the domineering, perfectionist Joe drilled the boys in dancing and singing during rehearsals. Joe Jackson had played in a rhythm and blues band, The Falcons, and wanted the next generation to have the success he hadn't.

And they began to show potential.

His mother holds on to more pleasant remembrances. Michael was born, she said, "with a funny-looking head, big brown eyes and long hands. He was special." She recalls him dancing, at 18 months old, to the rhythm of the washing machine. "There was something different about him. You know how babies move un-coordinated? He never moved that way. I don't believe in reincarnation, but – he danced like he was an older person."

Michael has spoken of her kindness. "When I was little, this bleeding man knocked on everybody's door early in the morning. Finally he banged on our door. Mother let him in at once." Of his early singing, he's suggested, "I was just singing in a baby voice and imitating sounds. I didn't know what the words meant, but the more I sang, the better it got. I always knew how to dance. I would watch Marlon because I could keep up with him as he was only a year older than me."

By 1964 Jermaine, Jackie and Tito formed the first incarnation of The Jackson Brothers, with two local friends on guitar and drums. Within a year Marlon, six, and Michael, five, had joined, playing tambourines and congas. Michael was not to stay in the background for long. His mother heard him singing while making his bed one morning. At a Garnett Elementary School recital in Gary, his first public performance, he moved his classmates and teacher to tears and won a standing ovation when singing "Climb Every Mountain". He was placed on backing vocals duty, then, swiftly, lead vocals,

"While performing and making music undoubtedly remain as some of my greatest joys, when I was young I wanted more than anything else to be a typical little boy," he was to recall many years later. "I wanted to build tree houses, have water balloon fights and play hide-and-seek with friends. But fate had it otherwise."

Born August 29, 1958, the seventh of nine children, Michael Joseph Jackson and his siblings experienced an extraordinary, turbulent youth. Parents Joseph and Katherine (*nee* Scruse) Jackson initially raised their working class family as Jehovah's Witnesses in Gary, Indiana, a small, hard, suburban industrial town. They lived in a two-bedroom clapboard house in a downmarket area. (The street was later named Jackson Boulevard in their honour.) They'd entertain themselves with songs and dancing. "The high school behind our house always had a big band with trumpets and trombones and drums coming across the street," mused Michael, "I loved that."

Joe was a former boxer and singer/guitarist, working as a crane operator for a steel company. Katherine brought up the kids – Michael plus Jackie, Tito, Jermaine, La Toya, Marlon, Rebbie, Randy and Janet – at home, singing them folk songs. But

PREVIOUS DOUBLE-PAGE SPREAD: The young star pined for a more carefree childhood.

LEFT: "Ben" was an unusual song about a rat – and an Oscar-winner.

RIGHT: The young Jackson 5 photographed in Chicago in 1968: Michael at the front.

alongside Jermaine. He'd studied the singing of Jackie Wilson, Sam Cooke, Stevie Wonder, Diana Ross; the moves of James Brown. "He was so energetic that at five years old he was like a leader," said Jackie in *Rolling Stone* magazine. "We saw that. And the audience ate it up." Joe scented a goldmine.

"We were really nervous rehearsing," Michael later said. "He sat in this chair and he had this belt in his hand. If you didn't do it the right way, Dad would tear you up, really get you. He was tough. There were times he'd come to see me and I'd start to be sick." He added, another time, "He seemed intent above all else on making us a commercial success. He was a managerial genius and my brothers and I

owe our professional success, in no small measure, to the forceful way he pushed us. Under his guidance I couldn't miss a step. But what I really wanted was a Dad." Driven on relentlessly by Joe Jackson, the boys debuted at Mr Lucky's nightclub in Gary, then hit the road across the American mid-West, as warm-up act in African-American clubs, burlesque palaces, even in less-than-glamorous strip joints. Their energy and talent soon won over any skeptics who'd looked at their age and scoffed. They'd earn whatever tips were tossed on stage. Part of Michael's job would be to crawl around the floor scooping up coins, filling his pockets. But not for long. Professional gigs followed. Michael was given his own solo routine mid-set,

LFET: Michael with mother Katherine and father Joseph.

RIGHT: Happy families? The September 24, 1971 cover of *Life* magazine shows the boys with their pushy parents.

before his eighth birthday. His offstage shyness would vanish the moment he stepped under the lights. In 1965 they won a local talent contest at Roosevelt High School, singing the Temptations hit "My Girl". Tito's school orchestra teacher suggested the name The Jackson Five. "It was really Tito who decided we should form a group," said Michael. "And we did, and we practised a lot, and then we started entering talent shows and won every one we entered."

Don Cornelius, creator of influential TV show *Soul Train*, was a Chicago radio D.J. in the mid-Sixties. He told *Time* magazine how he first felt the impact of Jackson live. "He's only four foot tall, and you're looking at a small person who can do anything he wants to do onstage – with his voice or with his feet. To get to the level of the people who can do that, you're talking about James Brown as a performer. You're talking about Aretha Franklin as a singer. Michael was like that as a kid. He could do it all, within the framework of one package. Nobody else did that."

Michael told Oprah Winfrey, "I thought James Brown was a genius. I used to watch him on television, as a boy, and I used to get angry with the cameraman because whenever he would really start to dance, they'd be on a close-up, so I couldn't see his feet. I'd shout, 'Show him! Show him!' so I could watch and learn." Michael's kindergarten teacher Gladys Johnson told reporters, "When he was five

years old and had difficulty with his arithmetic, he told his teacher, 'Oh, I don't need to learn those numbers. My manager will count my money.' At the same tender age he announced, "I would like to be a great entertainer. I want peace for the world. And I'd like to own my own mansion one day."

As a major step towards achieving these dreams, The Jackson Five landed their first record deal with local label Steeltown. They released their first two singles in 1967, both regional hits. These were "Big Boy" and "We Don't Have To Be Over 21 (To Fall In Love)". The first black boy-band were starting to make a name for themselves. They caught the attention of legendary soul duo Sam & Dave, of "Hold On I'm Coming" and "Soul Man" fame, who got them a coveted slot at the annual amateur night competition at the Harlem Apollo Theatre in August 1967. They won, of course. Soon they opened for Gladys Knight & The Pips, already part of the dazzling Motown Records roster. Gladys, a truly great singer herself, was impressed, and recommended them to Motown supremo Berry Gordy Jr. (Later, Gordy initiated the myth, for publicity purposes, that Diana Ross "discovered" the boys, but it was Knight who first urged him to check them out.)

The Jacksons' parents now pushed as hard as ever. If Joe was labeled the tyrant, Katherine was no shrinking wallflower. They were both aware that a child star's market-worthy clock is ticking fast.

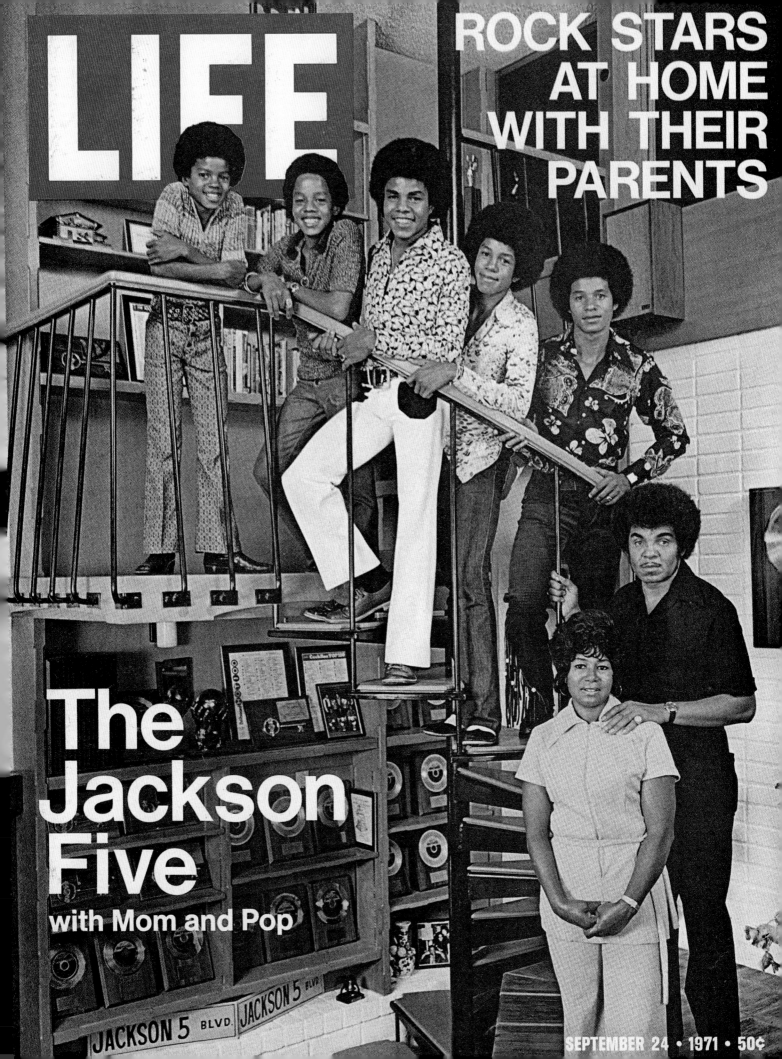

LIFE

ROCK STARS
AT HOME
WITH THEIR
PARENTS

The
Jackson
Five

with Mom and Pop

JACKSON 5 BLVD. JACKSON 5 BLVD.

SEPTEMBER 24 • 1971 • 50¢

"Katherine knew the only way out of Gary, Indiana was Michael," a family friend once said. "She turned to me and said, "Michael is cute now, but he won't stay that way forever – then what do we do? They've got to get a record contract now." Michael himself, even this young, had business acumen. He'd even organized a re-shoot of the photo session for the Steeltown release, with the label's president Ben Brown recalling that Michael had positioned himself at the front, saying this was "business", not "a family portrait". "He had some savvy," said Brown. "He knew even then."

And yet he was far from content. As he was to tell Oprah Winfrey, "It was lonely... having to think about popularity and all that. There were great times with my brothers, pillow fights and things, but I always used to cry from loneliness. I was very little – eight or nine." On another occasion he said, "I grew up in a fishbowl." The choreographer Vince Paterson has said, "Sure he's a little afraid of people. When you have people that from the time you're a little kid,

want a part of you, want your clothes, want your hair – you're going to get a little nervous around people."

Berry Gordy, meanwhile, was also concerned about the Jackson boys' age, having already signed one teenager in Stevie Wonder. He was worried about the then strict child labour laws. But the brothers continued to wow crowds and individual Motown musicians, and Berry was stunned by a videotape of their live performance. Soul singer Bobby Taylor had also been spreading the word. An audition with the label was set up in July 1968. Amid a full confident set they gave a blazing rendition of James Brown's
"I Got The Feelin'". Gordy sat poker-faced but knew he had to sign them. Later he confessed that he was thinking as he watched that Michael's dancing was too mature for his boyish, piping voice, and that he'd struggle to come up with material that was an appropriate fit. "We could not believe this old man in this young kid's body," he said.

He offered the contract Joe and Katherine had hoped for. They signed to Motown on July 26. Buying them out from the Steeltown label, he moved the boys and their father out to California and put them into the Hitsville USA studio in 1969. Michael, along with Marlon, was temporarily housed with Diana Ross in her mansion: the pair remained close friends for life.

LEFT: Michael sings on *The Sonny and Cher Comedy Hour* in July 1972.

RIGHT: Aged 13, Michael seen singing at home in Encino, California.

The Jackson Five became The Jackson 5, rehearsing feverishly, while the press department plotted their campaign (sometimes reducing Michael's age from eleven to eight) and fed out the story that Ross had discovered them. There was around-the-clock work, rehearsals and then more rehearsals. Songs and sound were honed. The look, the style, the clothes were crafted. Motown had set its very own handling team – The Corporation – the goal of getting these boys primed and ready for stardom. "When I look back on my childhood," Michael nevertheless later wrote, "it is not an idyllic landscape of memories."

Diana Ross introduced them formally to an audience of 350 invited guests on August 11, 1969, at the Daisy Club, Beverly Hills. TV appearances followed, and then, on October 7, the debut single, "I Want You Back". By January 1970 it was top of the charts. The group were to enter the new decade as America's number one, with their debut album *Diana Ross Presents The Jackson 5* also selling over a million copies. The Michael Jackson story had well and truly begun.

GOT TO BE THERE

Berry Gordy's Tamla Motown label – named after the "motor town" of Detroit, where former car assembly worker Gordy had started up the label, was already the stuff of legend. It pioneered and popularized African-American expression, fostering racial integration, and possessed an alchemical knack with a pop song, creating many of the most durably moving soul and dance records of its or any era. Motown brought black music from the ghetto to the mainstream. Among its great artists were Smokey Robinson, Marvin Gaye, Stevie Wonder, The Four Tops, The Temptations and Diana Ross & The Supremes.

PREVIOUS PAGE: All dressed up: The Jackson 5 line-up of 1977. Back: Marlon, Jackie; Centre: Michael, Tito; Front: Randy.

LEFT: The Jackson 5's million selling 1969 debut album *Diana Ross Presents The Jackson 5*. Gladys Knight actually saw the band before Diana.

RIGHT: Young, gifted and black: (l to r) Tito, Marlon, Jermaine, Michael, Jackie.

Gordy not only relocated Joe Jackson and the boys to California – where many of his business interests now lay – but moved Joe, Jermaine, Tito and Jackie into his home. The younger Michael and Marlon became house guests of Diana Ross. Michael and Diana became confidantes and Michael once said he shared his "deepest, darkest secrets" with her. (While he confirmed later writing the song "Muscles", named after his pet snake, for her, debate continues as to whether "Dirty Diana" was named after Ms. Ross). Gordy set up a PR exercise with Diana – Gordy's amour – introducing the group to the public. Thus they were granted the full beam of the Motown hierarchy's blessing.

Immediate dividends were reaped, as "I Want You Back" topped the US charts at the beginning of the Seventies. During 1970 The Jackson 5 were to enjoy no fewer than four number ones, thereby becoming the first group in pop history to go to number one with their first four singles. And the first Motown act to have four number ones in a year. There can be no doubt that "I Want You Back", "ABC", "The Love You Save" and "I'll Be There" are all vibrant, inspired records. (In the UK, incidentally, battling for teenagers' attention with the likes of Donny Osmond and David Cassidy, these four singles reached number 2, number 8, number 7 and number 4.) Their debut

album peaked at number five Stateside.

"I Want You Back" stamped Michael's voice and presence on the world's consciousness. The Jackson boys traded lines, calls and responses over an irresistible, joyous rhythm, but it was Michael, fronting the group onstage and onscreen, who stole the show. The moment where the small boy soars in with "Oooh baby, give me one more chance" announced a singer to match any of Motown's vocal giants. In April, the hyperactive and equally catchy "ABC" kept the momentum going. It knocked The Beatles' "Let It Be" from the number one spot. "The Love You Save", another warm jet of joie de vivre, topped the charts in June, and in October the touching, tingling ballad "I'll Be There" followed suit. To this day "I'll Be There" remains a vocal and melodic treasure. At age 12, Michael Jackson had sung a touchstone torch song. "I'll tell you the honest-to-God truth," Michael once admitted. "I never knew what I was doing in the early days – I just did it. I never knew how I sang. I didn't really control it. It just formed itself." It was there.

The Jackson 5 were labeled "bubblegum soul". Their influence on pop was immeasurable. Writer David Ritz called these singles, "moments of incandescent beauty – young and wildly optimistic.

They make us happy." Jacksonmania swept the States, coast to coast. Michael himself was made happier when his mother and sisters were able to join the rest of the clan in California. With success ensured, the family was reunited, moving into a large gated mansion in LA called Hayvenhurst.

It is perhaps easy to almost forget now that Michael Jackson, rising to prominence as the Seventies kicked in, was the first black superstar of the post civil-rights era. In an America with the potential and for the most part the desire to integrate, his success showed that it was possible to cross over peaceably. Chaka Khan once said, "That was a special time. We were all hopeful and seemed to be getting along in a way like never before. There was this wonderful feeling about being alive." The young Jackson was not politically active, of course, but his cultural ascendancy, and that of most Motown acts, was perceived and understood to be a product of benign developments. There were black pop groups on television, and to black families this made more sense,

and was more entertaining, than the Osmonds or the Partridge Family. The Chicago-raised academic and writer Bonnie Greer has written, "I understood viscerally the way they [The Jackson 5] dressed, what they referenced in their music and dancing. They belonged to me, to us, from the same background. Michael's family was not rich, except in their prodigious talent and work ethic. You could latch on to Michael – because he was African-American, because he was a black kid from a rough, blue-collar steel town."

While the Jackson 5's records' appeal transcended skin colour and age, Motown focused their marketing at the younger generation. The band had re-established Motown as "The Sound Of Young America". (Michael spoofed Frank Sinatra's "It Was A Very Good Year" on Diana Ross' TV show). A range of merchandise was promptly launched, from posters to patches. An animated cartoon series – *The Jackson 5ive* – featuring the band's "adventures" was broadcast on Saturday morning television.

LEFT: The young Michael Jackson in reflective mood.　　　　**ABOVE:** For Michael, singing was as easy as ABC.

And the boys starred in their own hugely enjoyable TV specials, such as *The Jackson 5 Show* and *Goin' Back To Indiana*.

Their schedule was by now punishing, and Michael, not even a teenager, could not walk down the street without being mobbed. When not travelling to or playing concerts, or TV slots, they were in the recording studio. In the space of six years, between 1969 and 1975, they made a staggering 14 albums. On top of this, from 1972, Michael was sidelining in solo releases. Not everything was sunshine and light. Michael found his new world strange and disorientating. He had to pretend to be asleep when his older brothers brought girls back to hotel rooms,

and despite all the acclaim he already had self-esteem issues. Enduring adolescence in public, he fretted about acne and the size of his nose. He later said, "I think every child star suffers through this period – because you're not the cute and charming child that you were."

The colourfully-dressed brothers' first European tour began in October 1972, with an appearance at the Royal Variety Command Performance at the London Palladium. They also played Wembley Arena (then Wembley Empire Pool) and charmed TV viewers on the BBC's *Top Of The Pops*. They were eager tourists, finding time to check out Buckingham Palace and 10 Downing Street. A review in *The Times*, before

LEFT: The boys on *The Ed Sullivan Show*, December 1969. Ed shakes Michael's hand.

RIGHT: Skywriters: (l to r) Michael, Jermaine, Tito, Jackie, Marlon.

criticizing the high ticket prices, noted, "Fourteen-year-old Michael has an astonishing command of gesture... his twinkling feet scarcely seemed to touch the stage."

The twinkle-toed one wasn't allowed time for rest and reflection. The hit machine kept functioning. Just some examples: in 1971, "Mama's Pearl" and "Never Can Say Goodbye". In 1972, "Lookin' Thru The Windows" and "Santa Claus Is Coming To Town". In 1973: "Doctor My Eyes", "Hallelujah" and "Skywriter". Moreover, Michael's solo albums *Got To Be There* (1972) and *Ben* (1973) were successful both musically and commercially.

"Got To Be There", a psalm sung by a yearning angel, was the 13-year-old Michael's debut solo single in the fall of 1971. It sailed to number one in the US, number 5 in the UK. His father and Gordy obviously recognized his potential, but the prospect of performing without his brothers was daunting for him. The album of the same name came out in January 1972. Although The Jackson 5 were still very much a viable concern, it was clear to industry insiders which way the wind was blowing. Michael

was now the biggest teen pin-up in the world. Good as the other Jackson boys were, they seemed, compared to this blazing talent, mortal. As the Motown ethic had the group choreographed and tailored as an ensemble, it was as if Michael was hemmed in, restrained, when lined up with his brothers. He'd keep bursting out of his chains, making it look too easy. He campaigned for more of a say. "Michael's always been different," said Berry Gordy. "He's more intense than anybody. He's made a science out of this." It was Gordy however who was making a science out of commerce in this period, and two best-selling recording acts for the price of one was his kind of moneymaker. With further hits like "Rockin' Robin" and "Ain't No Sunshine", it was only a matter of time before Michael's next number one. This came with "Ben", also the name of his second album of 1972.

What a strange song this was, and how weirdly prescient. A song about a boy's love for his best friend Ben, a pet rat, it was tied in with a creepy movie of the same name and won him an Oscar nomination. Let's not read too much into this: the track was originally written for Donny Osmond, but,

as Donny was on tour, was offered to Michael. Yet the cap fitted: Michael was already bringing unusual pets into the family home – peacocks, parrots, even a boa constrictor. "People come up and say, 'Why did you create a song about a little stinking rat?' laughed the star. "'How'd you make it so beautiful if it's about a dumb rat?'" There were further records, but Michael was changing, growing up as much as he ever would. His golden voice was breaking, but his appeal survived what had been a career-killer for many child stars. Puberty was, still, a challenge. He gained weight and became even more shy and insecure. His acne depressed him. He went on a vegetarian diet. The phase "messed up my whole personality," he later sighed. The difficulties of that time sowed seeds which haunted him and his perception of his appearance in later years.

"Whatever it took to get a song done right, he was willing to go the distance," producer Hal Davis observed of the young Jackson. "That was impressive. He was still just a little kid." Ever brave on stage, he learned to perform without his brothers around him, singing "Ben" live at the Academy

Awards. He still didn't want to leave The Jackson 5. They, however, wanted to leave Motown. This was a shock. Behind the smiles, however, there was growing acrimony between the family and Berry Gordy. They wanted more creative control, and quit the label in 1975. Michael's only comment was, "We didn't like the way we were being recorded." It may have had more to do with the pressures of promotion, the over-zealous studio calendars. 1974's "Dancing Machine" had shown the brothers were able to take up the challenge of disco, and weren't going to be left behind as it displaced old-school soul on the radio airwaves. And on the 1973 album *Get It Together* that the single was lifted from, they'd come up with some interesting, novel directions. But Gordy in this case was erring on the conservative side, not wanting The Jacksons to mature.

Their thrilling rendition of "Dancing Machine" on *Soul Train* moved *Time* magazine to declare, "It was an altogether funkier Michael Jackson doing the singing. Midsong, his face went blank as he popped through a jaw-dropping dance move called 'the robot'. It was his own invention, the product of

long hours of cunning physical engineering, nothing borrowed from James Brown." The song was a hit and the "robot" dance became a craze. "And," continued *Time*, "Michael Jackson was done being a prodigy and was on to something bigger."

When the breakaway came, Jermaine stayed at Motown, having married Berry Gordy's daughter Hazel, but Randy joined the band full-time. With a new deal signed with CBS (later Epic) Records, and a (legally-obliged) name change to The Jacksons, the family group had plenty of energy left. Image makeovers and international hits continued, as if to prove to Gordy that they could thrive as a tight unit without his backing. Over subsequent years they made the transition from pop group to well-rounded live band that could fuse pop, funk, soul, dance and ballads with consummate fluency. They focused more on albums than singles, working with classy writers/producers like the Philadelphia legends Kenny Gamble and Leon Huff. 1976's first album, *The Jacksons*, included Michael's debut as a sole-credited writer, "Blues Away". The slinky

Gamble/Huff number "Show You The Way To Go" gave the brothers their first British chart-topper (after a run of top ten hits). Second album *Goin' Places* was also Philly-influenced. By 1978 Epic trusted the Jacksons to produce themselves, and the million-selling *Destiny* was a vindication of that trust. It yielded hits like "Blame It On The Boogie" and "Shake Your Body (Down To The Ground)", with Michael now co-writing, an indication of how much his ear for grooves and melody had developed. Turning 20, he was close to finding the sound that would change R&B and pop forever. There were to be other significant Jacksons albums – 1980's *Triumph*, 1984's *Victory* (the latter marking Michael's final full sessions with the band) – but Michael was to make his move. It seemed the spell of being part of a group had been broken. He was something else.

His star was to rise with a velocity that would leave even his brothers blinking, like the rest of the watching world, with disbelief. Things were about to get very off the wall.

LEFT: By November 1978 The Jacksons had their own TV special. (L to r) Tito, Jackie, Michael, Marlon, Randy.

RIGHT: Michael fronts the brothers on CBS show *The Jackson Five*.

BELOW: Little Randy (left) joins the big boys on *The Sonny & Cher Comedy Hour*.

OFF THE WALL

"There is no way of preparing for success," Quincy Jones
has commented. "Especially the biggest success that ever
occurred in music history." By the late Seventies, Michael
Jackson was ready to go it alone and forge his own musical
path. Success beyond compare was imminent, but he
had to first experience a freakish one-off failure. On the
cusp of 20, he was cast in an acting role in *The Wiz*, an
expensive, African-American re-imagining of durable Judy
Garland movie *The Wizard Of Oz*. This new musical had
been a Broadway hit; everybody had high hopes for the
screen version. Michael was cast as The Scarecrow (who,
famously, had no brain). He worked hard, looked good on
camera, and the plan was that his agility and flexibility,
coupled with his infectiously cheery manner, would make
a perfect complement to his close friend Diana Ross as
Dorothy. Both singers were hugely popular. Also on board
were Richard Pryor and Lena Horne. Quincy Jones was
hired as musical supervisor and penned the score. Sidney
Lumet, one of cinema's greats, was to direct. What could
possibly go wrong?

PREVIOUS PAGE: A solo star is born: Michael at Madison Square Garden, New York.

LEFT: Jackson planned his first album "as a grown man".

ABOVE RIGHT: *The Wiz* cast Michael (left) as the Scarecrow. Diana Ross played Dorothy.

BELOW RIGHT: A 1979 studio shot, photographed by Jim McCrary.

Plenty. As this Dorothy and her crew danced from Kansas to the urban disco nightmare of New York, nothing quite gelled. Not the tone, not the songs, not the cast. It lurched between wise-guy humour and tear-jerking schmaltz. It was, in truth, an expensive folly and a bit of a mess, even if it was visually striking and imaginative. Michael's enthusiasm was abundantly clear. "I don't think it could have been any better. It was my greatest experience so far," he said. One critic hailed his "genuine acting talent."

The wonderful thing about this *Wiz* was that it introduced Michael and Quincy Jones to each other, and their yellow brick road was to be paved with gold. The versatile Jones had already enjoyed a formidable career, working with Frank Sinatra, Ray Charles, Aretha Franklin and Ella Fitzgerald as well as scoring numerous films. The pair struck up a friendship and Michael asked Jones to produce his first "proper" solo album – his first as a "grown man". For both it was a good move. "He wasn't at all sure he could make it on his own," said Jones. "And me too, at first. I had my doubts." Contributing songwriters included Stevie Wonder, Paul McCartney and the consistently under-praised Heatwave man, Rod Temperton. Jackson, who wrote three songs and co-produced three tracks, later declared, "When

"He wasn't at all sure he could make it on his own. And me too, at first. I had my doubts."
Quincy Jones

Quincy and I first started, we sat down and discussed exactly what we wanted and it's all tuned out the way we planned." *Off The Wall*, released on August 10, 1979, shaped the new Michael Jackson: the songs, rhythms, look and style that would make him the world's biggest star. It was the first solo album to spawn four number one hits in the US, went seven times multi-platinum there, and made him a household name around the globe. It was to sell twenty million copies, a massive figure – at least in pre-*Thriller* times. Its cover showed Michael grinning, sporting a tuxedo and the white socks that were to become a trademark. "The tuxedo was our idea for the project and package," said his manager. "The socks were his." *Off The Wall* was where Michael jumped over the wall, crossed the bridge from extremely impressive professional to inspired, out-there maverick genius.

Of his writing credits in general, Jackson's had the modesty to laugh, "I feel guilty having to put my name on the songs I write. I do write and compose them, and I do the scoring, lyrics and melodies. But still – it's a... it's a work of God!" Recording sessions had run between December 1978 and June 1979 in LA, at Allen Zentz Studios, Westlake Studios and Cherokee Studios. Jones feels they took many risks. When he called Temperton, he'd initially suggested he present three songs and they'd select the best one, but Jackson loved all three ("Off The Wall", "Rock With You", "Burn This Disco Out"). He completed the vocals to all three in two sessions, having stayed up all of the previous night to learn the lyrics by heart. This, he felt, meant he could throw himself into them without glancing at a song sheet every few seconds, could use his physicality. Temperton has said that he'd researched Michael's style in depth beforehand, and built up short-note, aggressive melodies to suit Michael's punchy technique.

From the first euphoric seconds of "Don't Stop 'Til You Get Enough" (written by Jackson in his kitchen, the story goes), you can hear the magic. As the man says, phrasing it perfectly – "Ooohh!" This, the first single, is an irresistible mix of disco rhythm (perhaps inspired by the Bee Gees' timeless *Saturday Night Fever* tracks) and soulful, urgent yelps, grunts, whoops and shrieks. Jackson was bold enough now to try out tricks that few other vocalists would dare to attempt. Reportedly his mother found it all a tad too "suggestive". Quincy was, correctly, encouraging him. "Everybody sang high at Motown, even Stevie Wonder," remarked the producer. "I wanted to feel the full range of his [Jackson's] voice; I wanted him to deal with some mature themes." Lust and music weren't a new combination, but this charged blend of desire and the sense of a higher power expressing itself hadn't been heard outside Al Green, James Brown and Marvin Gaye. Jones' strings interwove beautifully with the beat; the music collared you and instantly persuaded you to run with it, your body in motion. The writer Nelson George opined in 2004 that "the argument for Jackson's greatness in the recording studio begins with his arrangements (of this track). The layers of percussion and the stacks of backing vocals, both artfully choreographed to create drama and ecstasy on the dance floor, still rock parties in the 21st century."

"Rock With You" was an equally fluid and seamless slice of soul-swing. Justin Timberlake, about a quarter of a century later, has based most of his entire recorded output on the ideas in this cut. The title track "Off The Wall" is an effortlessly funky hymn to the liberating spirit of the disco boom. "Leave your 9 to 5 up on the shelf," he sings, "and just enjoy yourself." His own composition "Workin' Day And Night" – a stronger song than king songwriter McCartney's "Girlfriend" – is another disco fireball, to which it's impossible to keep still. The trembling "She's Out Of My Life" rewrote the rules on how to sing a ballad. Jones told *Time* magazine, "It was a song Tommy Bahlor wrote about a very bad ending to a marriage, and I was saving it for Sinatra, but I did it with Michael. Because I don't think he had ever dealt with an emotion that deep in a romance. And he cried on every take we did. Every take. I left the tears on the record because it was so real." Nelson George also eulogized this track. "It became a Jackson signature similar to the way "My

TOP: The King of Pop meets The King of The Ring (Muhammad Ali, with Veronica Ali) in 1976.

RIGHT: A still from Michael's 1978 studio shoot.

ABOVE: Jackson live in white tuxedo, working the crowd.

diverse as Liza Minnelli, Bianca Jagger, Woody Allen and Aerosmith singer Steven Tyler.

Less glamorously, he'd that year broken his nose during an ambitious dance routine, and underwent surgery. The operation wasn't an unqualified success: he complained of breathing difficulties and said they affected his singing. Further rhinoplasty and operations followed. This was the beginning of a slippery slope. Mother Katherine was also concerned. "He is quiet now," she said. "When he was younger, he wasn't so quiet. I think the stage might have done that. Wherever he goes, everyone is coming out to see Michael Jackson, to see what he looks like. He said he feels like an animal in a cage." For his part Michael was again telling interviewers that he was happier and more comfortable on stage than during everyday personal interaction. When one journalist inquired if he ever saw a day he'd retire from performing, he instantly laughed, "No way! Don't stop 'til you get enough!" Meanwhile, one of his old Motown tracks, the keening ballad "One Day In Your Life", was a surprise number one in Britain in June 1981.

One professional dancer commented on Michael's agility thus: "It's the combinations that really distinguish him as an artist. Spin, stop, pull up leg, pull jacket open, turn, freeze. And the glide where he steps forward while pushing back. Spinning three times and popping on his toes. That's a trademark and a move that a lot of top professionals wouldn't try. If you go up wrong, you can really hurt yourself." Michael is on record as saying, "When dancing, I felt touched by something sacred. In those moments I felt my spirit soar and become one with everything that exists. I became the stars and the moon, I became the lover and the loved."

Michael continued to undergo turbulent changes. His family relationships were now fraught. Upon turning 21 in August 1979, he boldly fired Joe Jackson as his manager. He replaced him with attorney John Branca, telling him he wanted to be "the biggest and wealthiest" star in the business. He bemoaned the (as he saw it) lack of acclaim for *Off The Wall*, saying it was "totally unfair that it didn't get Record Of The Year, and that can never happen again." He was also upset by what he perceived as racism. He offered *Rolling Stone* magazine a cover story interview in 1980, and when the decision was made not to go ahead with it, he remarked, upset, "I've been told over and over that black people on

Way" served Frank Sinatra. The vulnerability verging on fragility that would become embedded in Michael's persona found, perhaps, its richest expression in this wistful ballad."

Some claim Michael dedicated the song to Tatum O'Neal, the young actress who was reported to be his first girlfriend when he was just 17 and she was even younger. The daughter of Ryan O'Neal, she'd also experienced the highs and lows of child stardom. He however said that the relationship was just friendship, as physical intimacy "scared and frightened" him. "I really loved her", he recalled, "but I don't think I was ready for some of the things she talked about." Indeed Michael had been moving in more grown-up circles at this time, and photographs show him partying at New York's Studio 54 with characters as

LEFT: Jackson live in 1981.

RIGHT: Live and loved in 1981 – the crowd go wild.

BELOW: At the LA Forum with The Jacksons in September 1981.

the cover of black magazines doesn't sell copies. Just wait. Someday those magazines are going to be begging me for an interview. Maybe I'll give them one. And maybe I won't."

Michael did not always feel good when by himself, and the young performer was obviously finding the increasing pressures of international superstardom difficult to deal with. The lonely child star was becoming a lonely adult star.

"Even at home, I'm lonely," he confessed. "I sit in my room sometimes and cry. It's so hard to make friends... I sometimes walk around the neighbourhood at night, just hoping to find someone to talk to. But I just end up coming home."

Off The Wall, meanwhile, continued to woo the world, breaking records along the way. At the American Music Awards it won Favourite Soul/R&B Album, Favourite Male Soul R&B Artist and Favourite Soul/R&B Single (for "Don't Stop...") Surprisingly it only took one Grammy Award (his first since the early Seventies), for Best Male R&B Vocal Performance for "Don't Stop...", but took *Billboard* Awards for Top Black Artist and Top Black Album. The Grammy Awards were to loudly make up for their oversight next time around.

(As an added late extra, in 2008 they inducted this album into the Grammy Hall Of Fame). Yet their relative lack of enthusiasm here bothered the ambitious Jackson. "I wasn't too happy with the way it was accepted," he said. "I said, for the next album, I refuse to let them ignore me. I set my heart on it." As a lithe, lean, limber landmark which

(along with the Bee Gees) nailed the post-Motown disco mirrorball sound, with sophistication and sweat, *Off The Wall* merited every award going. (Jackson was also showing steely determination at home. He'd taken charge at the family estate in Encino, having it remodelled as a mock-Tudor mansion with a mini-replica of Disneyland's Main Street USA tagged on and countless animals now roaming the grounds.)

The place of *Off The Wall* in music history is

assured. In 2003 *Rolling Stone* listed it among the greatest albums of all time. "The album that established him as an artist of astonishing talent and a bright star in his own right," writes Stephen Thomas Erlewine in *Allmusic*. "This was a visionary album, a record that found a way to break disco wide open into a new world where the beat was undeniable." Other critics have hailed it as the work of a "blindingly gifted vocalist," with a "breathless, dreamy stutter." *Rolling Stone*, comparing his transition from young star to sophisticated performer to that of Stevie Wonder, suggested his "feathery-timbered tenor is extraordinarily beautiful. It slides smoothly into a startling falsetto that's used very daringly." Jackson's progression was universally recognized. In the UK, *Melody Maker*'s Phil McNeil called him "probably the best singer in the world right now in terms of style and technique." More recently *Blender* noted its prescience as "a blockbuster party LP that looked beyond funk to the future of dance music, and beyond soul ballads to the future of heart-tuggers – in fact, beyond R&B to colour-blind pop." Certainly Michael, whatever was going on away from studio and

TOP: Jackson's image was changing. A Lynn Goldsmith photo from 1979.

ABOVE: With Lionel Richie, "We Are The World" co-writer and lifelong friend.

RIGHT: Michael gave everything in his live performances.

"I've never seen anybody like Michael. He's an emotional child star, yet in full control."
Steven Spielberg

LEFT: *Off The Wall* established Jackson as a superstar.

BELOW: With Diana Ross at the 1981 American Music Awards.

RIGHT: Andy Warhol's portrait of Michael Jackson, 1984.

stage, was singing with what biographer J. Randall Tarborrelli called "joy and abandon".

"He is one of the last living innocents who is in complete control of his life," movie mogul Steven Spielberg once said of his friend. "I've never seen anybody like Michael. He's an emotional child star, yet in full control. Sometimes he appears to be wavering on the fringes of the twilight, but there is a great conscious forethought behind everything he does. He's very smart about his career and the choices he makes. I think he is definitely a man of

two personalities."

Jackson and Quincy Jones were to collaborate for a further fruitful nine years. In a way, *Off The Wall* was just another beginning in Michael Jackson's curious life of super-scale restarts, make-overs, reinventions, personality shuffles and conjuring tricks. He'd never hidden his wish to become the biggest name in the entertainment business, and when he and Jones regrouped in 1982 to construct his next magnum opus, that was his avowed aim.

Boy did he make it happen.

THRILLER

"We had a great team, a lot of talent, and good ideas", said Michael Jackson with an uncharacteristic degree of understatement. "I knew we could do anything. The success of *Thriller* transformed many of my dreams into reality." Its 42 minutes transformed the way music looked, walked and talked.

That transformation began in late August 1982 as the 23-year-old Michael re-entered Westlake Audio, Studio A, Beverly Boulevard, Los Angeles – where many of the *Off The Wall* sessions had taken place – to begin his new album. *Off The Wall* had established him as a grown-up R&B artist. This was to send his star into the stratosphere. So ambitious was he that, while everyone else concerned was patting themselves on the back, he felt disappointed that *Off The Wall* hadn't been even more successful. He was proud, shy and intense. He didn't like the media intrusion fame brought and yet, like so many since him, perversely pursued it. His family tried their best to circle the wagons around the golden goose, but, peeved with them, he was embracing business and management interests outside the clan. Even if the record industry was at this time in one of its downward sales spirals, he wanted everything about Michael Jackson to get bigger. He wanted to make, and be, a colossus.

"I wanted to do an album where every song was like a hit record," he said. "Why are some called 'album songs'? Why can't every song be so great that people would want to buy it as a single?" Before recording, he'd expressed a wish that "the next album has to be three times as great. It can't be just as good because that would be a let-down. So we'll take our time and get it right. I'm a perfectionist. I strive. I'll work until I drop."

The more experienced Quincy Jones remarked, "You can't expect the same kind of success that we had on *Off The Wall*, the market's changed," but Michael was adamant. His sights were set. He and Quincy were even more thorough concerning song selection than they had been on the previous album, sifting through hundreds of songs to find the very best. There were heated debates. "We turned that album upside down," said Jones. The quality control is indicated by the story that they even argued over "Billie Jean". Jackson loved the bassline and extended intro groove; Jones thought it too indulgent. "'Billie Jean' had an intro you could shave on, it was so long", said the producer. "I said, 'We've got to get to the melody quicker.' He said, 'But that's the jelly! That's what makes me want to dance!' When Michael

Jackson tells you that's what makes him want to dance, the rest of us have to shut up."

"I've never seen Quincy so into anything, ever," recalled studio engineer Bruce Swedien. "On the first day, he told us, "OK guys, we're here to save the recording industry." Lawyer and business adviser John Branca highlighted Michael's input. "Quincy, of course, did a wonderful job on these albums. Yet if you listen to Michael's demos for "Billie Jean" and "Beat It" you realize that he was actually the mastermind of those recordings." Jackson himself spoke of the near-obsession with perfection that fuelled the sessions. "We spent a lot of hours in the room working, 18 hours a day sometimes. We were sleeping on the couch. We'd wake up, mix some more, go back to sleep..."

"It was like he was going to make it this time or die trying," said Jones.

It's astounding to think this masterpiece, recorded in less than three months, was signed, sealed and released by November 30 of the same year, in time for the Christmas market. Jackson's duet with Paul McCartney, "The Girl Is Mine", had been (with hindsight) a surprising, misleading start-off single, released in mid-October, while the album was still being mixed. McCartney had said, "Michael originally rang me up on a Christmas day, and I didn't believe it was him. Eventually I said, 'Is that really you?' He was laughing on the phone, saying, 'You don't believe me, do you?'" The friendship between the pair was to suffer later that decade.

One CBS executive, Larkin Arnold, recalled a degree of worry. "The first mix sounded horrible. Quincy said, 'I can't give you this. We've got to do it all over again. I'll get it back to you in ten days.'" It was nerve-racking, but he did it." He had what Nelson George called, "snappy rhythm tracks and bright, immaculate arrangements." While the album was immediately popular, it didn't speed into its next gear until the following Spring. In February 1983 it made its home at the top of the *Billboard* chart and – already well on its way to being the biggest selling album of all time – didn't relinquish its spot for an incredible 37 weeks. (It frequently revisited the top again after that). Famously, as Jackson had intended, no less than seven of its tracks were top ten hits. The period between 1982 and 1986 earned Jackson over 700 million dollars. At one time the album was selling a million a week. And he got the Grammy recognition

he'd craved, winning a record-breaking eight in 1984. Significantly, these came in three separate categories: pop, R&B and rock.

It was the period where he became an icon beyond pop, patenting many iconic trademarks simultaneously. It wasn't just about the hits, incendiary as they were, but about his groundbreaking work in dance and on music videos. In both areas, he changed pop music forever.

In *Village Voice*, critic Vincent Aletti wrote, "In *Thriller*, Jackson has begun to part the shimmering curtain of his innocence – it's magic, it's unreal – to glimpse darker, deeper things. Once that curtain is ripped down, the view could be astonishing."

Before coming to the global phenomenon it was and the waves it made, let's look at the album itself. While it adds to the slick sounds of *Off The Wall* a few extra licks of rock and harder disco, its themes are often darker, touching on the supernatural and paranoia. Michael's love of tacky horror movies is evident but there's also a sense that some of the jittery unease bubbling under the surface stems from his own nervous tension at dealing with the constant spotlight of fame. As a writer he contributed to four songs ("Billie Jean", "Beat It", "Wanna Be Startin' Something" and "The Girl Is Mine"). It's been said that he didn't write anything down on paper; he'd just dictate words and sing melodies into a cassette tape recorder. With a budget of $750,000 the pressure was on (not least self-imposed to have hits), but the duet with McCartney "The Girl Is Mine", a mock argument over a girl, met a lukewarm reception, with some observers saying it blandly pandered to the white demographic. It took the second single, "Billie Jean", to clinch the deal. From then on things escalated, Jackson's video and TV appearances being global talking points. His multi-coloured music was breaking down racial barriers. He met with President Ronald Reagan at the White House, introduced the moonwalk, unleashed the epic, mindboggling "Thriller" video, and placed the young channel MTV on the map.

Everything begins however with the record. A record that, oddly, involved several members of soft-rock outfit Toto (of "Hold The Line", "Africa" and "Rosanna", fame). Jones was bringing choice musicians in, naturally, but he and Jackson, both caring about the project so much, still had intermittent rows. The mixes and remixes were, as

LEFT: "Billie Jean": another iconic video.

RIGHT: With *Thriller* producer Quincy Jones at the Grammy Awards.

mentioned, arduous. For one brief spell an emotional Jackson threatened to scrap the whole album. He was desperate to make sure that "every song is a killer".

"Billie Jean" – with Louis Johnson's gorgeous bass part hooking us in – in particular meant much to him, dealing as it did, daringly for the time, with the topic of obsessed stalker-like fans. One such weirdo insists Michael has fathered a child of hers. He disagrees. "She says I am the one/ But the kid is not my son". Said Quincy, "According to Michael, Billie Jean was about a girl that climbed over his wall. He woke up one morning and she was laying out by the pool, in a bathing suit. She'd just invaded the place, like a stalker. And Michael said she accused him of being the father of one of her twins...!" The song's an early sign of Michael's concerns about his celebrity status being as much a curse as a blessing. Fans were always hovering around Hayvenhurst.

Its video was unforgettable. Michael made the video age the new way of getting your music across to the masses, the ultimate means of searing your image and tunes onto people's brains. Before "Billie Jean", MTV was all but 100% white acts. Michael shifted that. "He totally defined the video age," said

Tommy Mottola, later head of Sony Music. "Nobody before or after Michael could do what he did for video. It put the MTV culture into the forefront." After Jackson, it was hard to hear a pop song without seeing the accompanying video's images in your mind's eye. And the great thing about the "Billie Jean" video is it's not particularly flashy. Its electricity is generated by Michael's own performance. As he moves, swaggering and shimmying, the paving stones his feet land on light up, glowing green. He struts, spins and physically portrays the song's beat and undercurrents, the embodiment of "feeling it". It may, by the way, be the best song he ever wrote, although there are some strong contenders for that title. And as Franz Ferdinand's Alex Kapranos has observed, "It's the best bass line ever written."

One weird, if commonly recounted, interpretation of "Billie Jean" is that it was written about Paula Abdul, Eighties pop star and now Noughties TV celebrity. It was alleged that she had an affair with Michael's brother Jackie. A choreographer, she hadn't at this point had a hit herself, although she was soon to do just that with "Straight Up", "Opposites Attract" and "Rush Rush", and later to work closely

"Maybe Michael will give me dance lessons one day."
Eddie Van Halen

ABOVE: Grammy master flash; Michael swept the board at the awards.

RIGHT: Out with his date, actress Brooke Shields, New York 1984.

with Janet Jackson on her videos.

"Beat It" also drew heated discussions. Jackson and Jones wanted a rock track that would endear the singer to the white rock fan market, and Van Halen axe hero Eddie Van Halen was brought in to provide an authentic shrieking guitar solo. Commented the musician, famously unpaid for the session, "Everybody from Van Halen was out of town and I figured: who's gonna know if I play on this kid's record? I didn't want nothing. I thought: maybe Michael will give me dance lessons one day. I was a complete fool, according to the rest of my band and my manager!" Jones remembered, "I called Eddie to play the solo. I said, 'I'm not going to tell you what to play, the reason you're here is because of the way you play.' So that's what he did. And he played his ass off."

The song was a tribute to – and, in less innocent times, a commentary on – classic musical *West Side Story* and its glamorized gang fights. "The point is," said Michael, "nobody has to be the tough guy. You can walk away from a fight and still be a man. You don't have to die to prove you're a man."

The track certainly proved its rock mettle to the equipment. During a playback the studio speakers caught fire. "Smoke," recalled assistant engineer Matt Forger, "came pouring out of the wall." "I've never seen anything like that in 40 years in the business," chuckled Quincy. Michael's red jacket in the video became another instant Eighties icon. The mini-movie reiterated the message that fleeing is wiser than fighting, as his character breaks up a ruckus by leading the gang members away to a spot of dancing. "I wanted to write the type of song that I would buy if I were to buy a rock song," said Jackson.

"Wanna Be Startin' Something" had been written a few years earlier and turned the heat up on the sound Michael had mastered on *Off The Wall* and on The Jacksons' better singles. Its bass and rhythms are fiendishly funky and its climax of a Swahili chant, sonically brave, is astonishing in its excitement and range. Jones persuaded Jackson to sing some overdubs through a long cardboard cylinder tube, adding innovative effects. Here he's already criticizing media gossip, a theme he'd return to often across subsequent releases. Understandably. Less explicably, he also posits himself as "a vegetable" on a buffet that fans can take a bite from. "Human Nature" is a beautiful, moody, introspective song, co-written by John Bettis, with Jackson's voice a tender treat as he croons, "Looking out across the morning/ the city's heart begins to beat/ Reaching out, I touch her shoulder/ I'm dreaming of the street…" His voice has more charisma than ever. He was now singing in a "fully adult style," noted *Rolling Stone*, that was "tinged by sadness." Stevie Wonder told *Time* magazine that when he first heard it, "I was over at Quincy's home and we danced to the music – it was magical." "Lady In My Life", another Temperton composition, was a soulful, sensual ballad, while the hypnotic "P.Y.T. (Pretty Young Thing)", a sleeper hit penned by James Ingram and Jones, was a delicious R&B nugget.

The grand guignol of "Thriller" itself, written by Cleethorpes' finest, Rod Temperton, had originally been called "Midnight Man" or "Starlight" in Temperton's mind, but he ultimately plumped for "Thriller", deeming it to have more unusual resonance and perhaps merchandising appeal as an album title. Its use of scary movie motifs, sound effects and vocal trembles – amid thunder, gales, footsteps, creaking doors and howling canines – cooks up the desired atmosphere of danger and drama. Then there's the Vincent Price-narrated section. "Rod was great," smiled Jones. "I called him on his way to the studio and he added this brilliant Edgar Allen Poe spiel that knocked our socks off." "When I wrote it," recalled Temperton, "I'd envisaged this talking section at the end and didn't really know quite what we were going to do with it. One thing I'd considered was to have a famous voice in the horror genre do a vocal piece. Quincy's wife knew Vincent Price, so he suggested calling him. I actually changed the lines in the back of the taxi on my way to the studio." Temperton saw Price stepping out of his limousine as his taxi arrived. He asked his driver to go around the back so he could grab a few extra seconds. Then he asked the secretary to quickly photocopy what he'd just written before handing it to the actor, the "king of the macabre". "Vincent sat down with it and got it in two takes." Some reports say Price (who Jackson had known since he was 11) was paid a flat fee of 20,000 dollars for his work. He was later given a gold record, but may have preferred a royalty. Because then the elaborate "Thriller" video, all 13 minutes and 43 seconds of it, upped the ante for the medium. At nearly $1 million, it was by a long way the most expensive video ever made at that time. Premiered on December 2, 1983, it was a horror-based miniature, part parody, part

chiller, directed by John Landis, who'd made *An American Werewolf In London*, a favourite film of Michael's. "I want to turn into a monster," the singer told Landis. "Can I do that?" Vincent Price's voiceover was just the take-off point for a whirl of spooky twists and terpsichorean zombie extras, an eerily-made-up Michael at the forefront. "It was," said Quincy Jones, accurately, "an event."

"I knew I wanted to do a short film," explained Michael. "A guy goes out on a date and confesses to the girl that he's different." So far, so Jackson. But the guy is, at least in her dreams, a werewolf. "I wanted to transform into different things." John Branca has recalled that Michael specifically asked for Landis, even though the director's price was sky-high. "With Michael there's nothing but business and bigness," one music industry bigwig has said. "Every new venture has to be bigger than Disneyland." This venture, if a gamble, was to be a roaring success.

"You're a hell of a mover." Fred Astaire to Michael Jackson

BELOW: Michael sporting the red jacket, which was to become an Eighties trademark.

RIGHT: Shooting the "Beat It" video, a modern take on *West Side Story*.

The "Thriller" video is established as a 20th Century art/commerce milestone.

Those werewolves and zombies were every bit as scary as Jackson had hoped. Hollywood effects and make-up legend Rick Baker reminisced, "Michael was very shy. The first time Landis came over to shoot us working on Michael's make-up, Michael was so nervous that he ran off and hid in the bathroom." The actress playing his girlfriend, one-time *Playboy* model Ola Ray, laughed that she teased him, "saying I wanted to be his girlfriend. He was cute, but child-like. He was back then nothing like the Michael of later. He loved to play, chasing me or jumping out from behind a wall." The famous dance sequences were shot on the underground concourse of the Rockefeller Centre subway stop in Manhattan, New York.

The video had a premiere cinema screening, at Michael's request. "It was incredible," Landis has said. Diana Ross and Warren Beatty were among the viewers. It received a standing ovation from the star-studded audience. They demanded an encore. Landis explained there wasn't anything else to show. "So show the goddam thing again!" yelled Eddie Murphy. Which is what they did.

If the future King of Pop was now the undisputed heavyweight champion of state-of-the-art music videos, he wasn't, perhaps surprisingly, embarking on a *Thriller* live tour. And yet it was an onstage moment that was to raise his fame, and the buzz around the *Thriller* era, up another notch. NBC were to celebrate the 25th Anniversary of Motown with a TV special on March 25, 1983. *Thriller* had been number one for what seemed like forever. Michael was invited to perform a medley with his brothers. A staggering 47 million viewers tuned in to watch. Motown itself had been wobbling a little in recent years, in terms of both quality and sales, but Berry Gordy cannily knew this would be a massive promotional boost. By making the event a benefit gig for sickle-cell anaemia, he made it difficult for the stars he was on frosty terms with to turn it down. Michael was also having his arm twisted by his brothers. Thus LA's Pasadena Civic Auditorium saw emotive turns from a reunited Diana Ross and The Supremes, Marvin Gaye, The Four Tops, The Temptations, Stevie Wonder, Martha Reeves and of course The Jacksons.

It was Michael who rendered the evening unforgettable. He was to undertake one more US tour

with the Jacksons, in support of their *Victory* album (which included a duet with Mick Jagger, "State Of Shock"), yet his heart had moved on. He knew he wanted to leave the group, having outgrown them, but had agreed to do the medley with them if he was then given a solo slot (as he was on the tour). He had something special planned for "Billie Jean". This was the night he introduced the moonwalk.

As his brothers drifted offstage after the medley climaxed with "I'll Be There", Michael, in a blue sequined jacket and one white glove, white socks visible under short black trousers, was handed a trilby. He began a routine which even the most sceptical of observers have described as poetry in motion. The moves, the dramatic static freezes, the lightning moves again. This was Jackson at his best. Even the older Motown gods and goddesses seemed awestruck.

Then came the Moonwalk. For a new generation it was their Elvis' pelvis moment, their Beatles' moptops moment. Strictly speaking, Michael didn't "invent" the move. Old-timers like Fred Astaire, Cab Calloway

and Marcel Marceau had created illusions of floating backwards, and in 1982 Jeffrey Daniel of disco group Shalamar had utilized it, as documented on *Top Of The Pops*. Michael had witnessed him on *Soul Train*, and one rumour suggests he asked Daniel to teach him the step. Yet Jackson, as was his way, took it further. His art was that of the magician. It was the very next day that the great Fred Astaire himself called him with congratulations, saying, "You're a hell of a mover. Son, you really put them on their asses last night. You've got rage in your feet. I'm the same way." Michael soon visited Astaire at his Beverly Hills home, and taught the 84-year-old how to moonwalk. (He later dedicated his autobiography, the appropriately-titled *Moonwalk*, to him). Another hero of Michael's, *Singing In The Rain* star Gene Kelly, called too, equally effusive. From that day on, schoolyards everywhere were suddenly full of kids dressed like Jackson, attempting to emulate his moves, calling him "the gloved one". Sales of the *Thriller* album went through the roof, worldwide.

Entertainment Weekly raved, "A delicate young man with a choked voice, a white glove and magic shoes... took the microphone and began to write the next chapter of American music history... squealing, moaning, spinning, taking the viewer's breath away... the music industry had to throw away its old yardsticks of success."

"When he did the Moonwalk at Motown 25," recalled John Branca, "that was a huge event. It led to the album selling a million copies the next week." Total sales were already tipping 25 million. "Everyone wanted to be like him," the R&B star Akon has said. "He was a kind of god in Africa." Sir Bob Geldof, who's said that Jackson was "a brilliant artist and a fantastic dancer," saw Jackson Moonwalk live at the Harlem Apollo that year. "On that hallowed ground, with the cream of black American music there, he performed "Billie Jean" and did the Moonwalk and it was gobsmackingly brilliant. The place just went wild."

It was now a landmark album, a monster bigger and more all-devouring than anything Jon Landis and Rick Baker could have dreamed up. 1983 saw "Billie Jean", "Beat It", "Thriller", "Wanna Be Startin' Something" and "Say Say Say" (with McCartney) dominating the singles charts. "P.Y.T. (Pretty Young Thing)" joined the club in 1984. As did sweet old Motown re-issues like "Farewell My Summer Love".

Jackson's ambition had been vindicated. The Grammy Awards concurred this time, making their 1984 event practically a tribute to him. His eight trophies – one being Best Children's Album for his work on Steven Spielberg's *E.T. The Extra-Terrestrial* – broke Paul Simon's record of seven, set in 1970 with the Simon & Garfunkel album *Bridge Over Troubled Water*.

Michael, dressed in full military uniform and aviator shades, chaperoned actress Brooke Shields and child actor Emmanuel Lewis to the ceremony. He denied any romance with Shields. "I took her to help her out," he said, perhaps rather ungallantly. "It was good PR for her to be seen with me." Brooke agreed. "We were just friends. He's nice. There was no great romance or anything." She added, "There were a handful of former child stars at the time. We were friends because we shared an understanding of how difficult life was in the public eye." Young Lewis was quoted as saying, "Michael is the best friend you could ever have. He's gentle, not rough like other guys." Neil Diamond congratulated him on achieving something neither of Michael's role models, James Brown or Diana Ross, ever had.

On top of the Grammys, Michael took eight American Music Awards and three MTV Awards. He was invited to the White House and on May 14, 1984 given an award for services to a charity that aided people in overcoming alcohol and drug abuse. (US transport secretary Elizabeth Dole had asked if they could use "Beat It" in a campaign to discourage teenage drinking.) "It was a lovely day," said John Branca. "President Reagan was very charming." First Lady Nancy Reagan offered this: "So peculiar! A boy who looks just like a girl, who whispers when he speaks. Who wears a glove on one hand, and sunglasses all the time. I don't know what to make of it." In fairness, she's also on record as saying, "Who knows how many lives were saved thanks to Michael's inspirational message, influence and songs?"

He was given a star on the Hollywood Walk Of Fame. He attributed it all, in a typically offbeat way, to his pets. "I love animals," he said in 1983. "I've got a llama, two deer, a sheep called Mr. Ted and all kinds of birds and swans. And a snake called Muscles." (The snake being the inspiration for the hit he wrote for Diana Ross). "I think nature and animals are very inspirational to my work. The majority of my success comes from that. I just play off life." (Bubbles the chimp, by the way, wasn't adopted until 1985.) Wry

LEFT: The now famous Moonwalk wowed even Fred Astaire and Gene Kelly.

BELOW: After the *Victory* tour with the Jacksons, Michael had to focus on his solo work.

LEFT: After visiting Madame Tussauds in London, Michael draws a huge crowd of admirers.

RIGHT: Shining like a star: Michael at the Grammy awards in 1984.

studio engineer Bruce Swedien said, "OK, so he has some animals. We're all crazy about animals."
He added, "OK, so he has had his nose changed a bit. That's just normal in LA."

Not everything went according to plan. Michael took a big fee to shoot a Pepsi Cola advert (even though he refused to drink it), against the advice of both Paul McCartney and Katharine Hepburn, who said it would cheapen his image, but during the filming in LA his hair caught fire. The expensive pyrotechnics had got out of hand. The commercial's director Bob Giraldi (who'd helmed the "Beat It" video) reported that he suddenly became aware that Michael was trying to tear his jacket off, thinking the flames had spread. "It was over before it started," he reckoned. But fire extinguishers were involved, and rescuers had to wrestle Michael to the ground. The media coverage was riddled with hysteria, as was to be the case for the rest of Michael's life. Michael, on being told that there were TV cameras outside as he arrived at hospital for a precautionary check-up after this incident, donned his white glove so that his wave from the stretcher would be more photogenic. Quite the showman, considering his head was bandaged and he did actually suffer second degree burns that

many claim ruined his hair forever. Although many criticized the artist's decision to take part in the Pepsi ads, specifically his endorsement fee of $15 million for three years, and he was accused of diva-like tantrums on set, one article described them as "a whole physical catechism of cool."

The eccentricity was to become a sticky part of the Jackson brand, would not overshadow the music, the videos and the bright-burning charisma. He had taken crossover fame to a new level. He was revered by people of any colour and creed, as long as they had ears and eyes. Commonplace as it is now, black R&B and white rock had never been fused into a globally popular sound before, certainly not by a big star and certainly not so effectively. His choreography was imitated everywhere. He wasn't perceived as predominantly black, or white: he was perceived as Michael Jackson, transcending such matters.

He was at his peak.

"Jackson is the biggest thing since The Beatles," declared *Time*. "He is the hottest single phenomenon since Elvis Presley. He just may be the most popular black singer ever."

"His new attitude gave *Thriller* a deeper emotional urgency than any of his previous work, and marked another watershed in the creative development of this prodigiously talented performer," wrote Christopher Connelly in *Rolling Stone*. He called it a "zesty LP with a "harrowing, dark message." Several critics recognized "Human Nature" as perhaps the album's best song, if not the most trumpeted. American journalist Robert Christgau rated *Thriller* as "almost a classic". He didn't like "The Girl Is Mine" but commended it for "getting interracial love on the radio". *Time* noted a year after release that, "The pulse of America and much of the rest of the world moves irregularly, beating in time to the tough strut of "Billie Jean", the asphalt aria of "Beat It", the supremely cool chills of "Thriller"."

Often overlooked is Jackson and his management team's business acumen around this time. John Branca has claimed that he obtained the highest ever royalty rate in the business up to that date, with the star receiving in the region of two dollars for every CD sold. It's been reported that Jackson rang his people every day, demanding more promotional pushes, and cried when *Thriller* finally slipped to number two. A tie-in documentary, *The Making Of Thriller*, funded by MTV, sold close to half a million within months. There were mounds of memorabilia and merchandising, including Michael Jackson dolls (selling at 12 dollars apiece). *Thriller* had, as Quincy Jones had initially said in jest, saved the record industry. *Time* magazine wrote, "the fallout from *Thriller* has given the music business its best years since the heady days of 1978... a restoration of confidence..." It hailed Jackson as "Star of records, radio, rock video. A one-man rescue team for the business. A songwriter who sets the beat for a decade. A dancer with the fanciest feet on the street. A singer who cuts across all boundaries of taste and style and color too."

An anecdote in Darwin Porter's book *Jacko: His Rise And Fall* has Michael Jackson meeting veteran crooner Frank Sinatra, who congratulates him on his success while offering sage words of caution. "Kid, the press will build you up today, because they like to tear you down tomorrow. In show business, you're hot and then oblivion. Very few entertainers can make a successful comeback. I'm the comeback kid. Frankly, I thought you were washed up in the Seventies. But who would have predicted *Thriller*?" Interviewed by Mark Ellen of *Smash Hits* at Christmas 1982 – his last British interview – Jackson claimed over the phone

that he did NOT like scary movies because "I can't sleep after watching one", and declared a love of old MGM films and stars like Katharine Hepburn and Spencer Tracy, as well as *E.T.* "I mean," he said, "who don't want to fly?" He also professed a liking for The Beatles (especially "Yesterday"), Simon & Garfunkel, Elton John and Adam & The Ants. "I still live with my folks," he said. "I'd die of loneliness if I moved out. Plus, I couldn't control the fans and stuff. I'd be surrounded."

LEFT: Ronald and Nancy Reagan invited a sharp-dressed Jackson to the White House.

ABOVE: The moonwalker, moonlighting during a Pepsi Cola commercial.

LEFT: On the Jacksons tour, playing Madison Square Garden in 1984.

ABOVE: With the legndary Paul McCartney, friend and collaborator on many songs.

Thriller WAS the Eighties. On February 7, 1984, it was inducted into the *Guinness Book Of World Records* as the planet's best selling album. It was in the top ten for 80 consecutive weeks, and America's best seller of both 1983 AND 1984. It has sold over four million in the UK. Popular R&B's domination of the singles charts to this day is largely down to the waves it started. As recently as 2003 it was ranked number 20 on *Rolling Stone's* list of the greatest albums of all time, though fans would surely rate it higher. In 2009 MTV Base and VH1 voted it the best album released in MTV's lifetime. It's been preserved by the US Library Of Congress as an item "deemed culturally significant".

Got that right. Worldwide sales of – latest figures claim – over 109 million copies pay testament to its ubiquity. The Rev. Jesse Jackson saw fit to praise its relative wholesomeness. "No dope-oriented album ever sold as much as *Thriller*," he announced, "and no vulgar artist ever became so famous as Michael has."

And it wasn't, like so many products of that decade, diminished to comic camp as the Eighties became a nostalgia act. A remastered special edition was reissued in 2001, including bonus material and Jackson's original demo for "Billie Jean", and in 2008 the 25th anniversary was marked by the release of *Thriller 25*, with remixes by modern-day fans like Kanye West, will.i.am, Fergie of Black-Eyed Peas and Akon. A bonus DVD included that Motown 25 moonwalk. And even this reissue went to number two in the US and number three in the UK, going gold in 11 countries. *Thriller* again sold in huge numbers after the tragic events of June 2009.

But right now Michael Jackson was very much alive, and probably the most famous man on earth.

This is how he is best remembered.

He was Moonwalking tall.

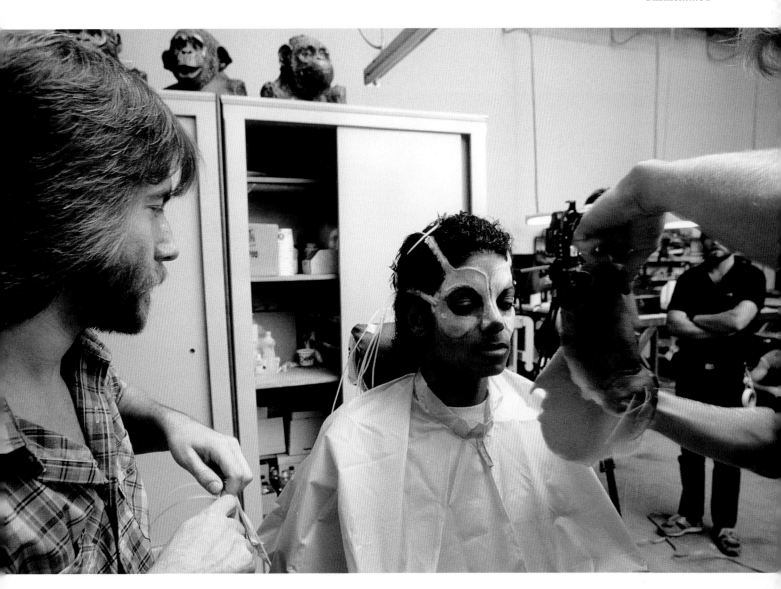

LEFT: Famous celebrity photographer Douglas Kirkland was given full access to the set of the "Thriller" video. The beautiful images over these six pages are photographs he took.

ABOVE: Michael spent hours getting made up for his various guises in the shoot, which was the most expensive video ever made at the time, at $500,000.

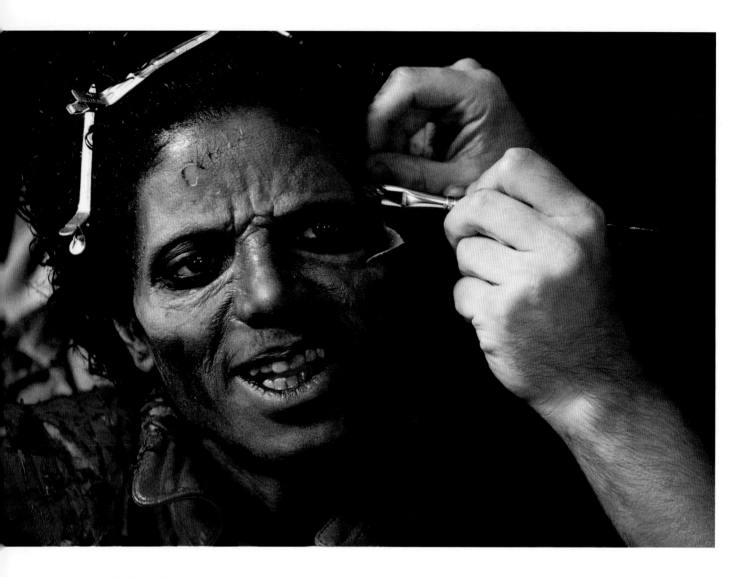

ABOVE: The Academy Award winning Rick Baker assisted with Michael's prosthetics for the video.

ABOVE: Michael was transformed into a member of the undead as well as a "cat-monster" during the video, which was prefaced with the statement, "This is no way endorses a belief in the occult."

ABOVE: Director John Landis had made the cult movie *An American Werewolf in London* two years before the "Thriller" video.

RIGHT: The video won two Grammies (Best Video, Long Form in 1985 and Best Video album for *Making Michael Jackson's Thriller* in 1984) and four MTV awards.

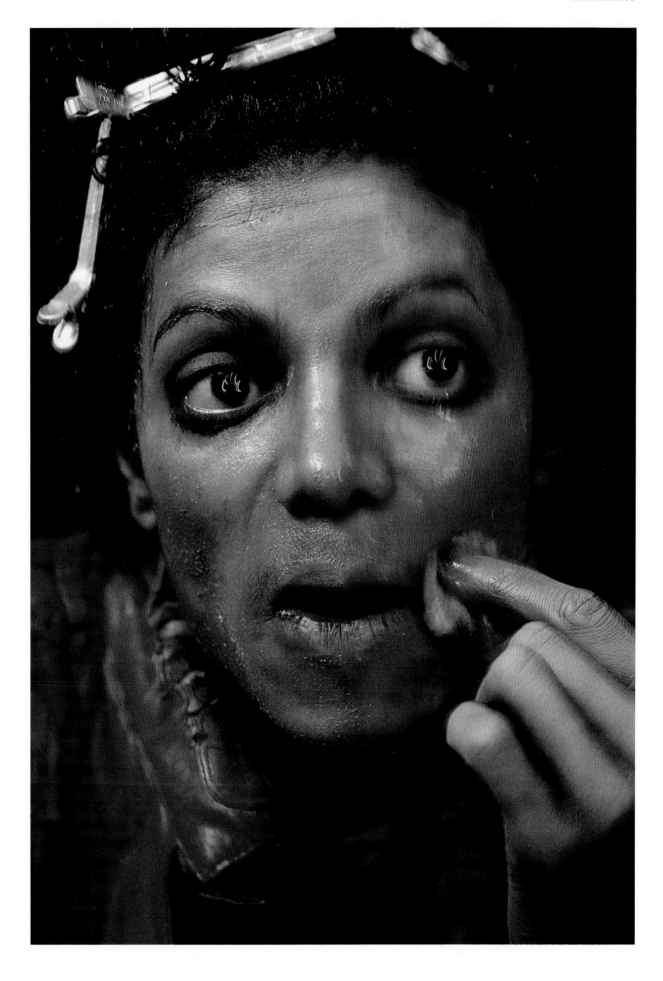

BAD

In 1985 Michael Jackson adopted Bubbles, a three-year-old chimpanzee rescued from a cancer research clinic in Texas. He would dress Bubbles in the same military-style clothes as himself. He'd take him to parties and press events, and claimed to have taught him how to moonwalk. It was around this time that Michael's eccentricities began to attract as much attention and debate as his music. Perhaps more. At first it was all great publicity, often generated by Jackson and his team, but it ballooned to the point where it lost any contact, however notional, with reality. There followed the increasingly unnerving changes in his appearance, the rumours that he wanted to buy The Elephant Man's or Marilyn Monroe's bones, the story that he slept in an oxygen tent.

After *Thriller*, his skin began to lighten. He insisted it was caused by the pigmentation disorder vitiligo, but some newspapers talked of "bleaching". Plastic surgery resulted, over the subsequent years, in his nose becoming thinner and sharper, his eyelids being raised, his lips shrinking and his chin suddenly revealing a cleft. There's an argument that the moment the "Wacko Jacko" headlines began to take over is the moment the erosion of Michael Jackson began.

PREVIOUS PAGE: The *Bad* tour saw Jackson adopting a tougher, rockier look.

RIGHT: Michael as a smooth criminal on the *Moonwalker* set.

ABOVE: "We Are The World". The star-studded cast of performers on the USA for Africa single.

LEFT: Michael with Bubbles the chimp.

Right now though he was on top of the world, looking down on sensation. In November 1984 he'd received a star on Hollywood's Walk Of Fame. Soon after that America watched, impressed, as the unlikely hero Bob Geldof inspired Band Aid and "Do They Know It's Christmas?", raising millions for famine relief in Africa. Naturally the USA wanted to have a go too, so in January 1985 Michael and Lionel Richie wrote "We Are The World". This they did within 12 hours of the idea being initially proposed. Almost every major singer in the States was roped in to the studio in LA to contribute, on the night of the American Music Awards (during and after the ceremony). Most were in

Hollywood for the awards show, and nobody wanted to be perceived as the uncaring curmudgeon. Michael skipped the show to sketch out the chorus with Quincy Jones, who produced. It's not easy to write a song that every kind of voice from Bob Dylan to Diana Ross to Dionne Warwick to Kenny Rogers can tackle, but "We Are The World" just about pulled it off. For many, Michael's regal vocal entrance, over the bridge, is the shivers-down-the-spine moment, highlighting him as the equal of any vocalist there. Among those soloing vocalists: Stevie Wonder, Paul Simon, Tina Turner, Billy Joel, Willie Nelson, Bruce Springsteen. Several Jacksons, Bob Geldof and one Smokey Robinson were credited

as extras on the chorus. The USA For Africa (United Support Of Artists For Africa) record, a worldwide number one and another Grammy winner, raised fifty million dollars for the cause.

Harry Belafonte had been a prime mover in making the song and session happen, after a nudge to America from Geldof, and it was Quincy Jones who sent Michael and Lionel Richie's demo to various singers, advising them all to "check their egos at the door". The response was huge, and about 50 huge stars had to be turned down. Among these was country star John Denver, who'd been actively campaigning against world hunger for several years. Madonna chose to pass. While most artists arrived by limo after the awards show, Springsteen drove a pick-up truck. Jones selected the performance order, often pairing male/female couples on the basis of how he figured their voices would match. He originally hoped to pair Michael with Prince (thinking it might dilute their perceived rivalry), but Prince neglected to

turn up on the day, so Michael sang with old friend Diana Ross. Prince later phoned Quincy Jones to offer a guitar part, but Jones told him it wouldn't fit. The Minneapolis man, clearly guilt-stricken, contributed a track to the subsequent album, and took part in a linked live event. Bob Dylan was reportedly shy of singing in such a busily populated studio, and Stevie Wonder helped him out on piano. There were disputes over the lyrics, although "We are the world/ We are the children" remains one of Jackson's most recognisable, if cheesy, lines to this day. One re-take was required when the sound of Cyndi Lauper's jewellery clicking could be heard on the bridge.

Later that year, Jackson again displayed a good eye for business, if not for the sensitive nuances of friendship, when he outbid both Paul McCartney and John Lennon's widow Yoko Ono to buy The Beatles' song catalogue and publishing rights for $47.5 million. This clever move, making him owner of the ATV Music Catalogue, was to earn him about

£7 million per year for many years, but it somewhat soured his relationship with former collaborator McCartney, who was displeased for obvious reasons. To McCartney it must have seemed as if his crown jewels were being pilfered, or that Jackson was showing off with regard to who was the biggest/ richest pop star in the world. His later dalliance with Lisa-Marie Presley also brought accusations that he was egomaniacally annexing pop history to further the glorification of himself. McCartney and Jackson had worked together happily on hits like "The Girl Is Mine" and "Say, Say, Say" and also duetted on "The Man" for McCartney's *Pipes Of Peace* album. McCartney had been given no inkling of Jackson's intentions however, and was stunned to take a phone call from a reporter one day seeking his response to his friend's purchase. He checked with an industry contact. Not only had Jackson outbid McCartney

and Ono (who McCartney had tried to persuade to combine with him in an increased bid), he'd outbid CBS, the Coca-Cola Corporation and Warners. He had control over every Beatles song written and released between 1964 and 1971 – a veritable goldmine and a self-replenishing pot of prestige. "I've found the Holy Grail," he remarked.

A music business executive commented, "despite that little girl voice and oh-so-delicate manner, Michael Jackson is one hard-nosed son of a bitch in business." McCartney's shock was intensified when he learned that Jackson had taken out a $5 million insurance policy on the Liverpool legend's life. "My God," he said, "he'll make millions when I'm 64 and gone." In a masterpiece of understatement, McCartney later said, "Our friendship suffered a bit of a blow." He was even more disenchanted when Jackson, who would cover "Come Together",

ABOVE LEFT: Looking up, live in 1988.

ABOVE: A Lori Stoll photograph of Michael.

ABOVE: On the set while making the video of "Bad".

ABOVE RIGHT: Stunning imagery from the London leg of the *Bad* tour.

allowed Beatles songs to be used in commercials, most memorably "Revolution" in a Nike ad. "Jackson has trashed the reputation of The Beatles," grumbled McCartney. "He seemed so nice and polite when I met him. But he has a heart of gold. And I don't mean that as a compliment." Many years later, in the 21st century, the habitually affable McCartney was to give out mixed messages about his former friend, calling him "an unusual guy".

Jackson had also instructed John Branca to purchase the rights to psychedelic-funk outfit Sly & The Family Stone's records, so his business empire was booming. Further acquired rights included Dion & The Belmonts recordings (including "The Wanderer" and "Runaround Sue") and works by flamboyant rock'n'roller Little Richard (like "Tutti Frutti"). While this was going on, his mother Katherine had filed for divorce from his father Joe, said to be philandering again. Joe refused to move out

of the Encino mansion, even though he was reported to be spending Jacksons-earned money on his other women. Michael is said to have muttered sadly, "She'll never escape." Indeed her legal tussles ground to a halt, unresolved.

And if Jackson's relationship with McCartney was on the rocks, he had plenty of other A-list celebrity friends queuing up to bask in his radiance and benefit from glamour by association. Such is the Hollywood in-crowd way. Enamoured of "old-school" stars, he actively pursued the blessing of several, from Elizabeth Taylor (who was to become a long-term friend and is said to have coined the name "The King of Pop") to Ava Gardner, from Marlon Brando to Robert De Niro, from Gregory Peck to Charlton Heston, from Jane Fonda to Andy Warhol to Sophia Loren. Ronald Reagan once rang him for a chat. "Perhaps," drawled Brando, "he needed Michael's advice on how to run the planet."

Eventually, amid all the hullabaloo, Michael was able to focus on recording a follow-up to the mighty *Thriller*. Sessions ran between November 1986 and July '87 (with "Another Part Of Me" taken from an '85 session). *Bad* was released on the last day of August 1987, five years on from its all-conquering predecessor. The hype machine went into overdrive and *Bad*, which went straight in at the top of the *Billboard* charts and stayed there for six weeks, was to be the first album in history to

yield five *Billboard* chart number one hit singles. It did especially well in the UK (where it's still in the top ten biggest sellers ever). The event-video for the title track, outdoing even the *Thriller* videos, was a 17-minute epic directed by Martin Scorsese. *Bad* has sold over thirty million copies – not as many as the unique *Thriller*, but easily enough nonetheless to place it high up on the all-time best-sellers list. There are many who believe it to be a better record than *Thriller*. *Rolling Stone* magazine was among them,

LEFT: Michael with pet boa
constrictor – "Muscles"
– in September 1987.

RIGHT: Michael in glorious
form on stage.

calling it "richer, sexier". "*Bad* is the work of a gifted singer-songwriter with his own skewed aesthetic agenda and the technical prowess to pursue it," wrote reviewer Davitt Sigerson. "Comparisons with *Thriller* are unimportant, except this one: even without a milestone recording like "Billie Jean", *Bad* is a better record." In terms of image, the visuals reinvented Jackson, a long way now from the squeaky-clean teen idol, as a punkish, leather-clad, crotch-grabbing, dirty dancer. (This was not his first choice: he'd hoped for a much softer, more fey image but the CBS record company put their foot down. "It's called *BAD*", yelled head Walter Yetnikoff.)

The massive 16-month world tour in support of *Bad* sold out 123 concerts, playing to four and a half million people. At the time it was the biggest money-spinner ever, earning $125 million dollars. He broke another record with seven sell-out shows in front of a total crowd of half a million at London's Wembley Stadium. (There were 1.5 million ticket applications). John Peel, writing in *The Observer*, called the show "stupendous... resembling some futuristic, technological pantomime." *Forbes* magazine named Jackson in 1987 as the ninth highest entertainer in the world. Less narcissistically, he gave millions of pounds in donations to children's hospitals, orphanages and other charities, while underprivileged kids were invited to watch shows for free. (Over the second half of the Eighties, Jackson gave an additional £300,000 to the United Negro College Fund. The entire profits

from the single release of "Man In The Mirror" also went to charity.) And yet despite the mammoth audiences, the paradoxes of Jackson's nature remained. Quincy Jones said, "Michael can go out and perform before 90,000 people, but if I ask him to sing a song for me, I have to sit on the couch with my hands over my eyes, and he goes behind the couch. He is amazingly shy."

Michael's competitive streak came through again. As he celebrated his 29th birthday (he'd renounced the Jehovah's Witnesses faith, so could now enjoy birthdays guilt-free), he felt a need to surpass *Thriller*. His sister Janet had recently had a runaway hit with her *Control* album, and it was reported that he resented her sharing the limelight. "I want to be the only Jackson on the charts", he is said to have grumbled. But there were five years between *Thriller* and *Bad*, and if he wanted to rule the charts again the pressure was on him to come up with the goods. And this he did, as *Bad* poured out its stream of international hits: "Bad", "The Way You Make Me Feel", "I Just Can't Stop Loving You", "Dirty Diana", "Man In The Mirror", "Smooth Criminal", "Liberian Girl"...

Jackson himself wrote no less than nine of the eleven tracks (if you include the lyrically autobiographical "Leave Me Alone", which was added on to the 1988 CD release as a bonus). He'd been documenting ideas since the end of his last Jacksons tour in 1984. "Another Part Of Me" had

been used in the *Captain Eo* project of 1986. Quincy Jones, for whom this was to be the last of his three great collaborations with Jackson, helped him harness his excess of half-formed melodies and words into a conventionally-sized album. Only two songs were from outside writers. "Just Good Friends", on which Stevie Wonder sang with Michael, came from Graham Lyle and Terry Britten, while gospel adaptation "Man In The Mirror" was credited to Glen Ballard and Siedah Garrett. A track called "Streetwalker" nearly made the cut – Jackson supporting it – but lost out at the eleventh hour when manager Frank DiLeo voted for "Another Part Of Me".

Michael had hoped for other big name contributions on the album. He was concerned that rising superstar Prince was stealing his thunder, and was being seen as more "cool" by critics and fans. He felt a rivalry, and concocted a notion that he and Prince should duet on the track "Bad" to see who was the "baddest". He thought it'd be smart to build up the competitiveness between the pair for the media's benefit, then release the song as a coup de grace. He is said to have told Quincy Jones, "He could do all those James Brown imitations I used to do, and I could do my famous moonwalk." Prince

wasn't keen on the idea. Or the song, which, when Jones sent him a demo, he dismissed. He did later qualify the rejection with a public announcement that "it would be a hit with or without me on it". And Jackson seems to have lived with this, judging by his children's surprising names. Yet he was more hurt when Barbra Streisand turned down an offer to duet, on "I Just Can't Stop Loving You". She is alleged to have laughed that a love duet between the couple would be "unconvincing". Jackson's team then ran the idea past Whitney Houston and Aretha Franklin, who also passed. Jones suggested Michael's old friend Diana Ross, but at that time the pair were on bad terms, having rowed, and Jackson said, "Why would I want to revive her career?" Thus Siedah Garrett, an "unknown" discovery of Quincy's and co-author of "Man In The Mirror", got the role. Her only high-profile success prior to this had been her duet with Dennis Edwards, one-time Temptations man, on the terrific 1984 dancefloor hit "Don't Look Any Further". Media gossips were quick to report a romance between Michael and Siedah, who was two years younger than him. One headline blazed: "Jackson And Lookalike Mulling Marriage". The pair were in truth just friendly: Jackson's tricks on Garrett included having his employees frighten her with his pet snakes. Jackson would hire her as a singer for future tours, but became jealous when, having sung on Madonna records, she joined Ms Ciccone's touring band much later. Madonna had by then become another perceived "rival".

"I Just Can't Stop Loving You" was the surprisingly mellow first single from *Bad*. Both vocalists were in fine form. The more attention-grabbing title track followed. Jackson had a new head publicist, Bob Jones, once of Motown. He got to work. A TV special, *Michael Jackson: The Magic Returns* aired, becoming the sixth highest rated show of its week. And the video for "Bad" was filmed. Could it possibly live up to the works of cinematic genius that had announced Thriller's arrival? With Martin Scorsese at the helm, it had a shot. Scorsese of course was famous for classic films like *Taxi Driver* and *Raging Bull*, and quite the music fan. (Jackson favourite Spielberg had been offered the gig first, but was unable to comply.) Shooting took place over six weeks at the Brooklyn Hoyt Schermerhorn subway station. It begins in black and white, with Jackson cast as a kid who's left the ghetto for an education but now doesn't fit in with his gang back home. "You don't down with us no more," they taunt him. "You ain't down. You ain't bad." Then the monochrome switches to colour, and Jackson starts singing and dancing, wearing his black-leather-and-buckles *The*

Wild One biker gear, chains and fingerless gloves, and showering peace and unity among the street kids. Jeffrey Daniel, Michael's old moonwalking friend, was among the extras, as was future screen star Wesley Snipes. Daniel has said that *West Side Story* was again Michael's main source of inspiration. The shoot moved on to Harlem, where Madonna, filming her "Who's That Girl?" video nearby, took a break to check out the Jackson/Scorsese set.

While many loved the video, which cost two million dollars, others were disappointed by Michael's appearance. He looked whiter than ever and the shape of his face was startlingly different to that of the young man who'd given us *Off The Wall*. The crotch-grabbing was starting to become a habit, almost a tic. Even Quincy Jones asked, "Is his underwear too tight?" Yet it made an impact. TV shows chattered of little else but Michael's look, songs, videos. *Bad* netted a sales boost and Jackson merchandise was thriving. "The Way You Make Me Feel" was another vast video, in scale, budget and ultimately presence. Michael was inevitably "romantically linked" to its co-star, Florida-born dancer Tatiana Thumbtzen. She'd beaten hundreds of other auditioning girls to get the role, but was paid just four thousand dollars for her four days of work. She was however invited onto the *Bad* tour, and in a book documenting her experiences has declared an unrequited crush on her employer. The pair's kiss onstage at Madison Square

LEFT: In concert in California, November 1988.

RIGHT: With Princess Diana in the UK.

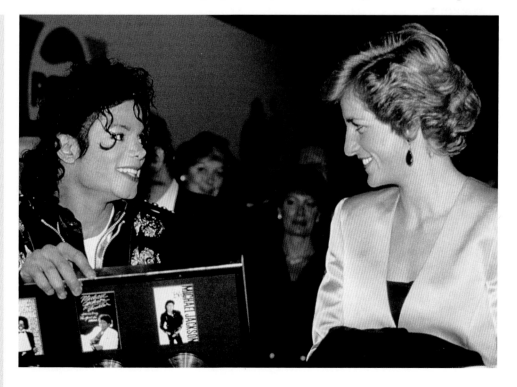

Garden in New York had newspapers calling her "Michael's Girl". Manager Frank DiLeo was cross with her – after all, nobody had seen Michael being kissed by a girl before – but, she claimed, Katherine Jackson gave her "a big bear hug". She thinks the security crew took a dislike to her, and she was sacked from the tour, to be replaced by a young wannabe named Sheryl Crow. Before long, the hungry media was saying that Jackson and Crow were dating. Tatiana went on to date Prince.

The marketing marched on. Jackson played a space captain, the title role in the short Francis Ford Coppola "sci-fi musical" film *Captain Eo*, produced in 3D by George Lucas of *Star Wars* fame, in which "Another Part Of Me" featured. At $20 million for 20 minutes, this was the costliest short ever made, and not the finest moment of Coppola, who'd made *The Godfather*, *The Conversation* and *One From The Heart*. It ran at the Disney Epcot Centre in Florida until 1994 however. It wasn't the epochal masterwork Jackson had hoped. While its place in cinema history is small, it was on a promotional outing for it that Michael first wore a surgical mask over his face, as an affectation. He'd been reading about Howard Hughes, the reclusive billionaire, whose story he found fascinating. He knew full well he'd be labelled as "bizarre", but didn't foresee how such stories would grow and self-perpetuate, spiralling out of control. In the *NME*, John McCready's review of *Bad* wryly began, "He bathes in Perrier water and wants to build his own Buck House. He asked David Hockney to paint Diana Ross' face on the bottom of his swimming pool. He hopes to live until he's 150. All these things are true. Such stories, created by an unholy alliance of Encino aides with a strange sense of loyalty but an innate understanding of the star system and a new dynasty of overpaid showbiz snoopers help convince a pop audience, for whom music is never enough, that Michael Jackson and the real world of alarm clocks and dirty socks do not belong together."

As "Dirty Diana" hit the charts, rumours ran that this soft-metal close relation to "Beat It", which featured a guitar solo from Steve Stevens, Billy Idol's sidekick, was Jackson's kiss-off to Diana Ross, with

whom he was now feuding. (They made up again in later years.) There were even reports that it was about Princess Diana. Stevens, wondering why Eddie Van Halen hadn't been called, wouldn't know, but he said of his session, "I ripped out a couple of solos, and he liked the first one. It was my choice too. He seemed to go on emotion rather than technique, which is how I've always worked."

As the icing on the cake of 1988 came a Michael Jackson movie, *Moonwalker*. The 93-minute film included renditions of "Smooth Criminal" and "Leave Me Alone" (each released as stand-alone videos) as well as "Speed Demon". It climaxed with a version of The Beatles' "Come Together". Directed by Colin Chilvers ("I expected it to be difficult," said Chilvers, "and it was. Michael's a perfectionist.") and Jerry Kramer, *Moonwalker* fanned the flames of what papers were calling "Jacko fever". Like *Captain Eo*, it was no *Citizen Kane*. A surreal blend of live concert footage, videos, Jackson biography, animation and cryptic, slightly eerie fantasy, it co-starred Joe Pesci (of Scorsese's *Raging Bull* and *Goodfellas*), 12-year-old Sean Lennon (John's son and for a while Michael's latest "best friend") as a "lost boy", and of course Jackson. It was pitched directly at true believers. Elizabeth Taylor and Mick Jagger could be sighted fleetingly. The singer had hoped to superimpose himself into a scene from a Fred Astaire movie herein, in a variation on a Ginger Rogers role, but Fred's widow denied permission. Jackson had dreamed of releasing *Moonwalker* in cinemas worldwide, but financial issues, even then, meant it made more business sense as a straight-to-video release. It was a gigantic hit, number one on the *Billboard* video charts for 22 weeks. And when it was knocked down to number two, its conqueror was *Michael Jackson: The Legend Continues*. *Moonwalker* had cost $27 million to make however, and so takings of $30 million in sales were less than satisfactory. Jackson was angry. He also wanted bigger sales for *Bad*, even though it was then the second biggest album of all time. Manager Frank DiLeo was fired, at Jackson's instruction, by his attorney, John Branca. It's said that Jackson also – irrationally – blamed him for allowing the "Wacko Jacko" nickname and image to stick. DiLeo later suggested that his former employer was "part Howard Hughes, part E.T.: Michael Jackson begs description."

The book *Moonwalk*, Michael's rather guarded

ABOVE: Michael starred as *Captain Eo* in Francis Ford Coppola's short film.

LEFT: Michael and manager Frank DiLeo arrive in England in 1988.

and idealized collection of memoirs and wispy thoughts, was initiated by former first lady and JFK's widow, Jacqueline Onassis. She was now a celebrity editor for New York publishers Doubleday. Doubleday knew that nobody, however famous, was unimpressed when they sent Jackie along to persuade them to yield up their stories. She insisted to Michael that millions of fans around the world would love to hear his tales. He protested that his life was only beginning. "Just be Peter Pan," she said, "that's all you have to do." When she flew to LA to meet him, he didn't turn up. Onassis was privately incandescent with rage. If anyone was as famous as Michael Jackson, it was her. Yet she persevered, and charmed him, as the pair compared notes on avoiding paparazzi. "Jackie twisted my arm," he said. Of Hayvenhurst, she commented, "It's La La Land. With a damn chimpanzee running amok. Animals in cages. Artefacts from the Land Of Oz." She saw the project through, however, with infinite patience (and a ghost writer). Although most reviewers reckoned the book gave up no secrets, Onassis wrote of her labour of love: "To many people Michael Jackson seems an elusive personality, but to those who work with him, he is not. This talented artist is a sensitive man, warm, funny, and full of insight. Michael's book, *Moonwalk*, provides a startling glimpse of the artist at work and the artist in reflection." Some of its passages did express Jackson's loneliness as a boy and mixture of pride and confusion as a man. Its most candid chapters confessed his troubled childhood and teased us with tales of life as 20 per cent of The Jackson 5. Indeed he phoned his father to apologize for the revelations. He also revealed here that he had had two rhinoplastic surgeries and a surgically-designed new cleft chin (having admired, in movies, the jawline of actor Kirk Douglas). The book, dedicated to Fred Astaire, topped the prestigious *New York Times* best-seller list, selling half a million copies in 14 countries.

For all this wide-ranging success, the Jackson backlash was knocking on the door. The *NME*'s John McCready wrote reasonably that, "*Bad* is a triumph of musical conservatism for a 29-year-old boy still trapped in *Off The Wall*'s disco inferno. If you don't think about the fact that it took the best part of five years to put together, then *Bad* is a good record." He

concluded, "That's all you can reasonably expect. Michael Jackson isn't God." *Rolling Stone*, however, in a poll of 23,000 readers, voted for *Bad* as worst album, worst single, worst hype, and worst video, and for Jackson as worst artist (and worst dressed). The magazine qualified this by saying it was his image, not his music, that got on people's nerves. The sheer scale of his fame was irritating them. But Jackson was even more irritated. He never forgave the publication.

Elsewhere, he was still revered and acclaimed. He took Brit Awards for Best International Male Artist and Best Video ("Smooth Criminal"). While the American Music Awards garlanded "Bad" as Best Soul/R&B single, Michael had mixed feelings at seeing sister Janet win Best Pop/Rock video for "When I Think Of You". He had high hopes however for another haul of gongs at the 1988 Grammys. Nominated for four, he – and the bookies – anticipated a sweep only slightly less triumphant than that of *Thriller*. As if to say thank you, he performed live at the awards ceremony, singing "The Way You Make Me Feel" and "The Man In The Mirror". This was his first onstage TV showing in five years. Standing ovations followed, and Quincy whispered in his ear, "The night is yours." But he won nothing. His pain was intensified as the Album Of The Year award was presented to U2, for *The Joshua Tree*, by... Diana Ross. The press claimed that he collapsed in shock backstage and accused the organisers of racism.

Bad, however, remains one of the most recognizable and dynamic albums made, and for many fans it's his very best work. (In 2001, a special edition was released with three new songs and a new booklet containing lyrics and never-before-seen photos.) "Man In The Mirror", with its incredible soulfulness, drama and vocal agility, may not have been the biggest of his hits upon first release, but after the saddening news of June 2009 it was the slow-burning song which, more than "Thriller", more even than "Billie Jean", seemed to catch the mood and serve as testament to the singer's unworldly gifts. Many news outlets quoted the song, as its poignancy captured both the moment and the man. "I'm starting with the man in the mirror/ I'm asking him to change his ways..."

As the Eighties danced towards their end, Michael Jackson had many more changes in store.

DANGEROUS

Michael Jackson, a boy in a bubble, retreated further into his own world by buying and converting the Neverland Ranch in Santa Barbara, California. He moved in in November 1988, his desires and idiosyncrasies requiring a place of their own away from Hayvenhurst and the Jackson family. Costing close to $30 million dollars then, the 2,700-acre (11 square km) property was soon decorated with a zoo (hosting, among many other exotic creatures, pythons and tarantulas), a Ferris wheel and amusement park, carousel, rollercoaster, dodgems, a cinema, and around 50 staff.

It was, Michael thought, a children's paradise. Here he could live out the childhood dreams the workaholic regime of Joe Jackson had never permitted him to have. He'd welcome young kids to come and play on the carnival rides. He'd named it after Peter Pan's island in J.M. Barrie's book; the world of never growing up.

Formerly the Sycamore Valley Ranch, Jackson's Narnia-like Neverland was about eight miles north of the nearest town, Santa Ynez. Its southern neighbour is Midland, a college prep boarding school. Jackson bought it from William Bone, a golf course entrepreneur. Other attractions included two railroads (with a locomotive train and coaches) and a floral clock. Michael had fallen in love with the ranch when visiting Paul and Linda McCartney there some time ago. (They'd considered buying it themselves, but it wasn't then for sale). When it did become available, he negotiated smartly over the price. Once in, he necessarily increased security and installed an imposing steel and iron gate with a giant gold crown atop it. He didn't invite his parents to his housewarming party, though various brothers and sisters came. Also there were Steven Seagal and Bo Derek. Confidentiality was asked for, though Michael

did tell friends, "I'm less than a 30-minute helicopter ride from Los Angeles. You can come visit me at any time." Frequent guest and child star Macaulay (*Home Alone*) Culkin said, "It was a child's dream, with every kind of soda in the world, every kind of candy. A two-floor arcade, a carnival, a movie theatre. We had very similar experiences in childhood. We're both going to be eight years old forever in some place because we never had a chance to be eight when we actually were."

The star's income was big but his spending was almost on the same level. He'd rarely question a price; he barely noticed if he splashed a six-figure-sum in one shopping spree. The basic maintenance alone of Neverland was $2 million a year (and rising each year). Right now it wasn't an issue. He was worth $1 billion at his peak, and earned royalties of $250 million in the Eighties. He'd also acquired some Elvis songs for his publishing catalogue. Added to the Beatles' songs, this was now worth $350 million. He was sitting pretty, but as the Nineties moved on his expenditure of an average of $30 million a year was to prove troublesome. After 2005, 17 years on from Neverland's conception, he decided not to return. He said he no longer considered it home, as the police had "violated" it during their intensive searches. Soon, to save on costs, the staff were let go and the facilities closed. Foreclosure proceedings commenced in late 2007, and legal proceedings wrangled on. Jackson still owned a stake in the property in 2008, but the amusement rides were seen being ferried along the road with a view to a sale. The brokenhearted Jackson's dream of 1988 was well and truly over. Upon his death there were reports that he was to be buried at Neverland, and that it would become a place of pilgrimage for Jackson fans, just as Graceland had become for Elvis. Logistics and legalities interfered, however, and his memorial took place in LA. Such sad times were as yet a long way off.

Michael wasn't at home as much as he might have

LEFT: Superbad on stage in Buenos Aires.

ABOVE RIGHT: "They ain't seen nothing yet", Jackson vowed as the Nineties began.

wished in 1988 anyway. His record-shattering *Bad* world tour was in full flow, boosting his profile to perhaps an even higher level than that attained by *Thriller*. People around the planet wanted to catch a glimpse of the near-mythical creature they'd witnessed in those groundbreaking videos. To see the moves and hear the voice for themselves. "For different people, growing up can occur at a different age", said Jackson himself, "and now I'm showing the world that I'm the man I always wanted to be." Certainly there was a harder, tougher edge to his music, wardrobe choices and stage presentation. There was an onstage power and aggression, dovetailing with the silky voice and

steps. The show utilized lasers and magic tricks, Michael displaying a love of theatrical illusion which may explain his friendships with Uri Geller and David Blaine. He'd hang suspended from a crane, high above the crowd, many of whom thought they were seeing a man fly. His seven spectacular shows at Wembley Stadium saw Prince Charles and Princess Diana in the audience. Michael joked to Charles, whose mother he'd once been introduced to backstage as a member of The Jackson 5, "I can give you some dance lessons." "Yes," smiled Charles, "I can be a bit awkward on the ballroom floor." Jackson had considered removing "Dirty Diana" from the set in their presence, for risk of causing offence, but didn't. Diana's reaction was positive. She got up and danced. Charles didn't. "I was so excited at meeting the royal couple," Jackson told reporters. "I'm very, very happy they came to watch me perform. I thought the Princess was wonderful." It's said that he and Diana spoke on the phone several times subsequently, comparing notes on avoiding the paparazzi and discussing clothes and style. Later, Michael would say of the doomed Diana, "In my heart I was saying, 'I love you Diana! Shine! Shine on forever because you are the true princess of the people.'" On hearing of her death in 1997, he said, "I collapsed. I fainted. I cancelled my show because I simply could not perform. I broke down and wept and wept for weeks afterwards. She used to confide in me. She felt hunted and trapped the way I do."

Around the time of this royal meeting, Michael sighed, "They call Elvis the King – why don't they call me that?" The moniker The King of Pop soon followed, often attributed to his close showbiz friend Elizabeth Taylor, though it may have been the insecure Michael himself who insisted it stick. Movie icon Taylor, a star from a young age herself, had once spoken of Jackson's interest in meeting other durable high-end celebrities. (Some claim he even proposed to her in the Eighties). "He is very curious and wants to draw from people who have survived... who have lasted the course. He is not really of this planet. If he is eccentric it is because he is larger than life. What is a genius? What is a living legend? What is a megastar? Michael Jackson is. And just when you think you know him, he gives you more. There's no-one who can come near him. No-one can dance like that, can write lyrics like that, or cause the kind of excitement that he does."

Jackson was already forced to don disguises if he wished to walk in the "real" world or visit a store, flanked by bodyguards. Yet onstage, as always, he was in his element. The *Bad* tour lasted from September 12, 1987 to January 27, 1989. It spanned 15 countries on four continents. For all its impressive financial tally, it actually cost Michael money. His deluxe lifestyle, stretching to private planes and helicopters, didn't come cheap, and the extravaganza

RIGHT: Jackson sports a codpiece for the Wembley Stadium concert of 1992.

that was the show itself provided multiple bangs for the audience's buck. Reviews were rarely dull. *Today* raved, "Raw sex". In Japan he was named "Typhoon Michael". Australia was more ambivalent, with the "Wacko Jacko" tag and jokes about the crotch-grabbing taking precedence over more layered analyses. Concerts in Perth and Adelaide were cancelled due to poor ticket sales. Michael wrote a hurt (and badly spelt) letter to *People* magazine, which said, "Do not judge a man until you've walked two moons in his moccasins." The British media riffed on the "Peter Pan of Pop" angle. All in all the tour was eventful, sometimes euphoric and sometimes exhausting. Even its starting date in the US had been argued over. Jackson planned to open in Atlanta, but his sponsors, Pepsi, thought it too closely associated with their rival, Coca Cola. So the tour began in Kansas City, where before the show Michael reportedly prayed, "Make us funky!" Afterwards, he was told the show had made three quarters of a million dollars, breaking the previous record set by... Elvis. One writer recorded that Michael danced happily and said, "Who's The King now?"

He still craved a movie breakthrough, but rumours of his casting in *The Phantom Of The Opera*, mooted to be directed by Steven Spielberg (but years later helmed by Joel Schumacher), came to naught. He appeared at awards ceremonies with Hollywood legends like Sophia Loren and Sylvester Stallone. He became friendly with David Geffen, the new mogul in town and the man behind new Hollywood studio Dreamworks (along with Spielberg and Jeffrey Katzenberg). The two spoke many times but Jackson's record deal with CBS was tight, to Geffen's dismay, and the right movie role for Michael couldn't be agreed on. "It's got to be Busby Berkeley meets *E.T.* with *Star Wars* as a backdrop," is one quote attributed to Geffen. When Michael failed to turn up for the opening of the Universal Studios Theme Park in Florida, the relationship suffered. Yet when Michael heard that the Rolling Stones' *Steel Wheels* tour had broken the takings records set by *Bad*, he fired his long-standing attorney, John Branca. Frustratingly for Jackson, he did this just as Branca was about to secure him the rights to James Brown's back catalogue. Geffen advised Jackson on a new legal and management set-up to replace those who'd guided him through his most successful decade. Sandy Gallin was the new manager.

One report claimed Michael was planning to buy out Motown Records. Berry Gordy Jr.'s catalogue was available for $200 million, but Jackson wasn't prepared to offer over $135 million. *The National Enquirer* announced his "romance" with Karen Faye, his make-up artist on *Captain Eo*. "He is a special person who has given me more in my life than anyone," said Faye. "It was the luckiest day of my life when this magical man sat in the make-up chair before me." The relationship with backing singer Sheryl Crow was also being blown out of proportion. The *Bad* tour party member would later go on to win nine Grammys herself in the late Nineties. "He never took off that glove for me," she said. The closest they got to romance was while singing "I Just Can't Stop Loving You" onstage. Then, on an even bigger scale, there was a reported date with Madonna. The media were alerted to a rendezvous at LA's The Ivy Restaurant. Madonna arrived dressed in black, Michael in white. They left in separate limousines. Apparently their competitiveness and jealousies – "Queen of Pop" Madonna's star was very much on the up – dominated the evening's conversation. They did attend the 63rd Oscars together, but this was blatantly a publicity exercise rather than any show of tenderness. "Jackson looked positively legendary in gold-tipped cowboy boots, a blinding diamond brooch and – in a dramatic sartorial departure – two gloves", recorded *People Weekly*. In Andrew Morton's Madonna biography, it's suggested that Madonna tried to seduce Michael "shortly after the Oscars. Nothing happened because he was giggling too much. That was one man she was not able to conquer."

The outgoing Eighties were nearly through. Michael was presented with the Artist Of The Decade Award by his confidante Liz Taylor. He watched The Jacksons' album without him, *2300 Jackson Street*, sell fairly poorly, and the Jacksons' deal with Epic came to a quiet end. The bigger record companies made it clear they weren't interested in putting up big dollars for The Jacksons unless Michael was involved. In December 1989 he was named Most Important Entertainer Of The Year by *Entertainment Tonight*. *Thriller* was chosen as Number One Album Of The Eighties by *Rolling Stone*. It had been, without doubt, his decade. Even President George Bush (Senior) wanted in on the action, and in April 1990 Jackson was invited for another visit to the White House where he was hailed as "Entertainer Of The Decade"

LEFT: Sinister yet scintillating: Jackson rivets an audience in Bucharest.

ABOVE: The King and Queen of Pop. Michael Jackson and Madonna looked an incredible couple on a night out.

LEFT: Accepting another award: in Monte Carlo for the World Music Awards.

RIGHT: Fellow snake-lover Slash of Guns'N'Roses plays on "Black Or White", live in Tokyo.

and honoured for his work for children's welfare.

Now the Nineties were coming. "The world likes to build a star up to tear him down," Diana Ross had long ago warned Michael. For his part, the singer was confident. "They ain't seen nothing yet," he allegedly told David Geffen. "I'll double my success in the Nineties." But times were about to get dangerous. 1991 saw Jermaine Jackson openly criticizing his younger brother. "I could have been Michael," he said. "It's all a matter of timing, of luck." He went so far as to release a single, "Word To The Badd", which took potshots at Michael's changing appearance. It ran: "Once you were made, you changed your shade/ Was your colour wrong?" Michael was furious and called his mother to complain, telling her to throw Jermaine out of Hayvenhurst, the family home which was still mostly owned by Michael. Katherine talked him down, but on the rare occasions Michael visited, Jermaine, who complained that Michael hadn't been taking his calls, was told to keep away. The two did make up in later years. "The overall message is an older brother telling a younger brother to get back to reality," Jermaine told the BBC. The very same week as "Word To The Badd" was released, Michael's own comeback single, "Black Or White", from the new album *Dangerous*, emerged. Unlike Jermaine's record, it shot to number one around the world, naturally.

Interestingly different to the previous three world-dominating Michael Jackson albums, *Dangerous* was released on Epic on November 26, 1991. It was co-produced by Jackson with 22-year-old Teddy Riley and Bill Bottrell, movers and shakers on the newly happening scene of "urban pop/R&B" or "swingbeat". Quincy Jones, stepping aside, had recommended their talents. Recorded between June 1990 and October 1991 at Ocean Way and Larrabee North Studios in LA, *Dangerous*, in tune with the compact disc (as opposed to vinyl long player) era, clocked in at 77 minutes, featuring 14 tracks. After the rock riff and anti-racism message of "Black Or White" kicked off, tracks released as singles in 1992 included "Remember The Time", "In The Closet", "Who Is It", "Jam", "Heal The World" and "Give In To Me". The album – a double on vinyl – went instantly to number one on the *Billboard* chart, and stayed there for four weeks. In the UK it beat U2's *Achtung Baby* to the top spot. Since then it has sold 32 million copies worldwide, 7 million in the USA, and been labeled "the most successful New Jack Swing album of all time." The sleeve illustration was an eye-popping piece of neo-psychedelia by Mark Ryden. Although it picked up just one Grammy (for Best Engineering, by Teddy Riley and Bruce Swedien), its sales in emerging markets like Asia and South America were even faster than those achieved by *Bad*. And Jackson's acceptance of the Grammy Legend award in 1993 sent it racing back up the charts. He was presented with this by sister Janet.

"See," he quipped, "me and Janet really are two different people!" There had been an early indication of the anticipation surrounding the new album. At LA International Airport three hundred thousand copies of *Dangerous* were stolen by a group of armed robbers, days prior to its official release date.

It was a fresh direction in many ways. In March 1991 the singer had signed a new agreement with Sony Music, which was reported as "a 15-year, six-album" deal. Wild sums as high as a billion dollars were said to have gone Jackson's way. These may have been exaggerated, but it seems agreed as fact that he won the highest royalty rate in the history of the business. By 2006 one calculation reckoned he'd earned $175 million from this deal from album sales alone.

Jackson performed at the 27th Superbowl half-time show in 1993 at the Rose Bowl, Pasadena, winning the event its highest ever audience: an incredible 133.4 million. With such colossal promotion, not to mention the *Dangerous* world tour (which was pitched as "the most spectacular, most state-of-the-art show the

world has ever seen"), it's little wonder *Dangerous* went seven times platinum. "Black Or White" was his biggest hit single since "Billie Jean". Jackson thus became the first artist to have number one hits in the Seventies, Eighties and Nineties. At the beginning of its campaign, Jackson was particularly pleased to hear it getting more radio play than Madonna's "Like A Prayer", the previous record-holder. This time round his rock guitar hero of choice was Slash of Guns'N'Roses. The accompanying video was of course an event, and its cost an astonishing seven million dollars. John Landis, who had made *Thriller*, was asked back to direct. He and Jackson had many creative disagreements. The theme of the song, and therefore the video, was clear: to encourage racial harmony and integration. "It don't matter if you're black and white." Among the faces blending in the video were Balinese, Sudanese and American Indian. The result was great, with a panther morphing (with the help of state-of-the-art CGI) into Michael. Such sleight-of-computer tricks were new and startling

at the time. 550 million people watched it. Jackson seemed fired up, using plenty of sexual and even violent movements within his gesturing. Indeed, after a meeting with Fox, scenes of him smashing the windows of cars and shops necessitated a Jackson public apology. "It upsets me to think that "Black Or White" could influence any child or adult to destructive behavior, either sexual or violent", it read. "I've always tried to be a good role model and therefore have made changes to avoid any possibility of adversely affecting any individual's behavior. I deeply regret any pain or hurt that the final segment of "Black Or White" has caused children, their parents or other viewers." This being a Michael Jackson story, the media kept the controversy going as long as they could. "He has really gone insane with this one," bleated one paper. Yet the record sold, and its call for unity resonated.

In October 1991 Michael hosted Elizabeth Taylor's eighth wedding, to Larry Fortensky, at Neverland. He escorted her down the aisle and happily met the bill of $1.5 million. Among the 170 guests were Ronald Reagan, Gerald Ford and Gregory Peck. His thankyou gift from Taylor was a rare albino bird. "Michael is the least weird man I know", said Taylor. Meanwhile work in support of *Dangerous* continued. The videos were never less than epic, with jawdropping dance routines and visuals. "Remember The Time" (dedicated to Diana Ross, with whom Michael was friendly again) took place in an ancient Egyptian palace, with longtime Jackson fan and sometime onstage mimic Eddie Murphy as a pharaoh and ex-supermodel Iman (Mrs David Bowie, as of April 1992) as his queen, who's attracted to Jackson's character. John Singleton of *Boyz N The Hood* fame directed. "In The Closet" co-starred another well-known model, Naomi Campbell, as Michael's lover. Directed by photographer Herb Ritts, it had a subtlety and sensuality lacking from some of the more broad,

ABOVE and LEFT: Michael on tour: the *Dangerous* shows were loud, colourful and exciting, even by Michael's high standards.

RIGHT: Michael takes time out from his hectic schedule.

ostentatious videos. It was genuinely sexy. However the song's lyrics – "Whatever we do now, whatever we say, we'll keep it in the closet" – kept gossips in fuel for months. And not just because Princess Stephanie of Monaco was credited as a backing vocalist.

"Jam", directed by David Kellogg, seemed consciously designed to make Michael appear more normal, as he played basketball with sports icon Michael Jordan and taught him how to dance. "Feel all your energy and... explode! Pow!" The two appeared genuinely happy exchanging lessons in their field of expertise. A video for "Dangerous" was shot by the legendary David Lynch (*The Elephant Man*, *Eraserhead*, *Mulholland Drive*) but is only available as a collector's rarity. And David Fincher, who went on to fame with *Fight Club*, and *The Curious Case Of Benjamin Button*, shot the video for "Who Is It". Jackson wanted to work with only the best, and generally got them.

The *Dangerous* tour was sponsored again by Pepsi, with the company paying Michael around $20 million. There were delays and cancellations, but it was intended to run from June 1992 to November 1993, with 3.5 million fans attending. Michael developed problems with his vocal cords however, so the tour stopped and restarted once or twice. It even visited Africa, where Michael hadn't been since he was a teenager. With another example of sound business savvy, Jackson's team also sold the film rights to the tour for $21 million. You guessed it, another record for its time. A Bucharest concert was filmed and shown on HBO in October 1992, drawing a gargantuan viewing audience. The touring entourage consisted of no less than 235 people, travelling on 13 customized coaches. Profits however went to his Heal The World foundation – which airlifted 43 tons of medical equipment to war-torn Sarajevo – and other charities.

Perhaps *Dangerous*, which cost a record $12 million to produce, lacked the great songs and feel that had so distinguished Jackson's work with Quincy Jones, but its more cutting-edge rhythms intrigued a younger generation. Teddy Riley said, "Thank God for Michael Jackson. He has helped me so much. These songs on *Dangerous* will determine how my career will be. Whatever happens I'll always have this." Riley also admitted that Jackson had talked a lot to him about the changes to his face and skin. "If he could do it all over again, he would

not have done what he did," he said. Co-producer Bill Bottrell shed light on the star's unorthodox way or working. "He hums things," he began. "He can convey it with his voice like nobody. Not just lyrics, but he can convey the feeling in even a drum machine or a synthesizer part."

Critical response was, as usual with Jackson, mixed. "How dangerous can a man be when he literally wants to please everyone?" asked the *Los Angeles Times*. They went on to dismiss it as "a grab-bag of ideas and high-tech non-sequiturs, with something for everyone from the man who has everything. Tame, unfocused." The *Independent* wrote, "The formula remains wearyingly familiar... all that's altered is the beats, pounding away in the foreground... Unable to face the fresh challenges of the Nineties, Jackson reiterates the clichés that

served him so well in the Eighties." Its experimental direction and impressive scope was overlooked by some. It was to be ten years until Michael would release another full album of all-new material. The review in *Q*, by Mat Snow, was more lively, accurate and positive, beginning, "Housed in a sleeve so symbol-laden that it could provide grist for an entire symposium of pop psychiatrists, *Dangerous* encompasses the entire range of what has come to be expected from Michael Jackson: aggression and schmaltz, paranoia and rose-tinted optimism, Godliness and megalomania, innovation and caution, the sublime and the ridiculous. Foremost, however, it offers danceability to an alarmingly intense degree." After noting the assertion of groove and rhythm over "the highs and lows that dramatise traditional pop" in the six opening Teddy Riley tracks, and pinning Jackson's vocals as "like James Brown's, gasps, squeaks and orgasmic shudders," the review nails "Heal The World" as "an insulin overdose... making The New Seekers sound like NWA." It concludes, "Great stuff... will he ever find true love and inner peace? What a star."

Michael's own words on the album weren't backward in coming forward. "I wanted to do an album that was like Tchaikovsky's *Nutcracker Suite*," he declared magnificently. "So that a thousand years from now people would still be listening to it. Something that would live forever. I would like to see children and teenagers and parents and races all over the world, hundreds and hundreds of years from now, still pulling out songs from that album and dissecting it."

"I want it to live on."

ABOVE: A lifelong fan, Michael pays homage to Charlie Chaplin in performance.

LEFT: Michael finds a quiet corner at Masada in Israel.

RIGHT: Posing for a thoughtful photograph session with Lynn Goldsmith.

SCREAM

Trouble and strife. From the early Nineties onwards,
Michael Jackson's life became even more turbulent. He
had never had a "normal" life, but now the spotlight grew
blinding. "Stop pressuring me", he pleaded, in one of his
most direct and candid songs, "Scream".

PREVIOUS PAGE:
Superstar couple: Michael
Jackson and Lisa-Marie
Presley together on stage
at the MTV Video Music
Awards in New York City.

LEFT: Michael and Lisa-
Marie make a charitable
appearance at a hospital for
children in Hungary.

Myths, gossip and rumours were everyday occurrences to him. From this point, however they were inflated to the levels of scandal and shock. Public opinion divided and polarized. He grew irate with one interviewer. "Why not just tell people I'm an alien from Mars?" he said. "Tell them I eat live chickens and do a voodoo dance at midnight. They'll believe anything you say, because you're a reporter. But if I, Michael Jackson, were to say, 'I'm an alien from Mars and I eat live chickens and do a voodoo dance at midnight', people would say, 'Oh, man, that Michael Jackson is nuts. He's cracked up! You can't believe a damn word that comes out of his mouth…'"

The changes in his appearance had fascinated some and dismayed and outraged others. "All of Hollywood has plastic surgery!" he protested. "I don't know why the press points me out. It's just my nose, you know." In 1993 came the crisis point. Allegations of child abuse were to throw him into a spiral of trials by media, trauma and excruciating embarrassment. His image took a battering. It was to be no easy decade, and his attempts at damage limitation, like his curious television interviews and a startling 18-month marriage to, of all people, Lisa-Marie Presley, only fanned the flames of controversy.

As the Nineties were finding their feet he was still enough of a superstar to be deemed relevant to a proposed brave new era. New Democrat President Bill Clinton and family invited him to one of the inaugural balls in Washington in January 1993. Clinton's daughter Chelsea was said to be "ecstatic" about meeting her pop hero. The singer led celebrities in a chorus of "We Are The World". With the *Dangerous* album proving he was still a powerful force in the market place, it seemed he was making the transition between decades solidly enough. But the Nineties were to be The King of Pop's nemesis. 1993 was his annus horribilis. He began it addicted to painkillers, for which he'd first developed an appetite after the accident on the Pepsi commercial shoot burned his scalp and hair. By November, Pepsi had withdrawn £35 million worth of sponsorship from a mooted tour, which was then cancelled, with Jackson, in his own words, "suffering great pain in my heart."

As the "Wacko Jacko" label stuck, he said sadly, "Wacko Jacko – where did that come from? I have a heart and I have feelings. I feel that when you do that to me. It's not nice. Don't do it. I'm not a 'wacko'." In February a rare, seemingly frank and decidedly curious televised interview with Oprah Winfrey saw him explaining the all-work-and-no-play difficulties of being a child star. "I used to always cry from loneliness. I didn't have friends. My brothers were my friends." Oprah asked if he had a tendency to escape into his imagination back then. "No," he said, "and that I think is why I compensate. I loved and still love show business, but then there are times you just want to play and have some fun, and that part did make me very sad." As well as claiming that he was still dating close friend Brooke Shields (he did go to the Grammys with her), he used this opportunity to retaliate at those who accused him of bleaching his skin in an attempt to become more "white". "I have a skin disorder that destroys the pigmentation. It's something I can't help, OK? When people make up stories that I don't want to be what I am, it hurts me." Despite this, he insisted he was "very happy".

Not for long. While fans stayed doggedly loyal, many shuddered as Michael Jackson was sensationally accused of sexually abusing a 13-year-old boy he had befriended, Jordan Chandler. "I'd slit my wrists before I hurt a child," he argued. "I could never do that. No-one will ever know how much these wicked rumours have hurt me." After mountains of publicity, the case never went to trial. He was to settle the claims out of court, paying the Chandler family a vast multi-million-dollar sum, the exact amount varying from report to report. The decision, possibly ill-advised, didn't put matters to rest: in fact the settlement meant the tongue-wagging and whispers only increased.

Jordan "Jordie" Chandler, born in 1980, 22 years Jackson's junior, had been a lifelong fan, learning the dances, wearing the glove. When they first met Jackson gave him a copy of *Dancing The Dream*, the coffee-table book published after *Moonwalk*. The two struck up a close friendship. Jordan was invited to Neverland with his mother and half-sister. Their host showered them with expensive gifts. Public displays of affection were to follow, including one in front of 500 million TV viewers at the World Music Awards in Monaco, where the two dressed in matching attire. Jackson was awarded the title of "World's Best-Selling Artist Of The Era". (He also started his own record label at this time, the MJJ label releasing the *Free Willy* soundtrack, with Jackson's song "Will You Be There?" as the theme song, as its debut).

After Chandler's family went to the police, and Santa Barbara prosecutors began an investigation into Jackson's activities, headlines blazed, "Is Peter Pan the Pied Piper In Disguise?" and "Is *He* Dangerous or just Off The Wall?" The police, with search warrants, raided Neverland, to the private singer's horror, and his Century City condominium. They hauled away boxes of "evidence" – photographs, videotapes. Jackson's criminal attorney Howard Weitzman called and heard the incredulous singer say, "I love children – the whole world knows that. How could they do this to me?" Early TV polls showed that only 12% of the public believed the accusations were true. Michael somehow completed a concert in Bangkok, but then cancelled the next, claiming illness. He upped his painkiller intake. He called Elizabeth Taylor, his ersatz mother figure. She and her husband flew to meet him in Singapore. "This is the most awful thing that could happen to a man like Michael who loves children and would never harm one of them," she told reporters. "I believe that Michael will be vindicated." She mentioned the word "extortion". Michael turned 35 the next day, a subdued birthday. He cancelled more concerts, suffering "migraines". His parents and brothers met him in Taiwan. He claimed he would never set foot in Los Angeles again.

Hollywood's glitterati at first rallied behind the singer. Expensive lawyers were however being hired by the Chandlers. Jackson's spirits revived sufficiently to march with Russian soldiers in Red Square. "Michael, Russia Loves You!" read a banner. Soon he took a break in Geneva with Taylor and husband. Then Buenos Aires. While lawyers exchanged verbal punches in LA, Chandler was grilled by psychiatrists and prosecutors. Jackson's legal team advised him to return to LA. He spent time in Puerto Rico and Mexico City instead, fearful of being arrested. On November 8, 1993, while many of the Jackson family were attending the funeral of Samuel Jackson, Michael's grandfather, police raided Hayvenhurst. This again drove Michael to despair. He got through his final concert, in Mexico City on November 12, then took a chartered jet to England, landing at Luton rather than London in the hope there would be fewer paparazzi there. He released an audiotape to the media.

"As I left on this tour", it said, "I had been the target of an extortion attempt, and shortly thereafter was accused of horrifying and outrageous conduct. I was humiliated, embarrassed, hurt and suffering... The pressure resulting from these false allegations coupled with the incredible energy necessary for

LEFT: The newlyweds: Michael and his new bride stepping out.

me to perform caused so much distress that it left me physically and emotionally exhausted. I became increasingly dependent on painkillers to get me through the tour... I realize that in order to regain my health completing the tour is no longer possible and I must cancel the remaining dates. I know I can overcome the problem and will be stronger from the experience." A publicist confirmed that the rest of the tour was off and that Michael's painkiller addiction had begun in 1984 after the Pepsi ad head-burning incident. A plan to record a theme song and appear in a video for the movie *Addams Family Values* was also dropped. *People* magazine ran the cover story: "Michael Jackson Cracks Up." Sony declared their "unconditional and unwavering support."

When he did return to LA, he flew in a jet owned by the Sultan of Brunei, a wealthy fan. Arriving via a circuitous route at Neverland, his heart sank upon seeing a crowd of TV crews, photographers and reporters. In 1994 he was strip-searched and photographed naked by police, calling it in a press statement: "the most humiliating ordeal of my life, one that no person should ever have to suffer. It was a horrifying nightmare. But if this is what I have to endure to prove my innocence, my complete innocence, then so be it." He concluded, "At every opportunity the media has dissected and manipulated these allegations to reach their own conclusions. I ask

all of you to wait to hear the truth before you label or condemn me. Don't treat me like a criminal, because I am innocent."

After much to-ing and fro-ing, a settlement was agreed and signed on January 25. Some put the figure agreed at $20 million dollars, others higher. Its cost to Jackson's image, pride and self-esteem was immeasurable. Months later, the star said, "I asked my lawyer if he could guarantee me that justice would prevail. He said there was no guarantee what a judge or jury would do. So I said that I have got to do something to get out of this nightmare. All these people were coming forward to get paid on these TV tabloid shows. And it's lies, lies, lies. It could go on for years. So I got together with my advisors and we made a unanimous decision to resolve the case." It wasn't until the next September that prosecutors made a final decision not to file criminal charges, with Jackson's accuser no longer willing or able to testify.

Jackson's lawyer said, "The time has come for Michael Jackson to get on with his life."

This was exactly what he had begun to do, as early as May 1994, when he married Elvis Presley's daughter. "I'm really learning the real meaning of love," he swooned.

Jackson and his latest flame were wed quietly on May 26 in the Dominican Republic. It was to be the only quiet thing about the marriage. The union of

The King of Pop and the heiress to The King of Rock 'n' Roll was, inevitably, catnip to the media. Many criticised a cynical P. R. stunt, designed to divert attention from Jackson's very public troubles and re-brand the perception of his sexual identity. The marriage may have been conceived as a shot at making him appear more "normal". In fact the celebrity status of both parties just sparked another frenzy of speculation. "Just think," mused Michael early on in the relationship, "nobody ever thought this would last." And it didn't, as Lisa-Marie filed for divorce, citing irreconcilable differences, in January 1996.

If anyone understood and grasped the strangeness of Michael's existence, it may well have been Lisa-Marie, who had seen at close hand the burdens and aftermath of fame so great that few could even imagine it, let alone handle it. Born February 1, 1968 to Elvis and Priscilla Presley in Memphis, Tennessee, an only child, Lisa-Marie lived at her father's estate Graceland – perhaps Jackson's inspirational starting point for Neverland – until her parents' divorce in

1973. She then divided her time between Graceland and her mother in Beverly Hills. She was used to luxury and attention at a very early age. Elvis' private jet was named after her. When Elvis died in 1977 (arguably the most momentous celebrity demise before Jackson's own), she lived full-time with Priscilla, but the mother and daughter often had a fractious relationship. Lisa-Marie claimed Priscilla was too often away shooting her TV series *Dallas*, and that her mother's boyfriend, Michael Edwards, made inappropriate advances. Lisa-Marie became something of a wild child: she was first married at 20, to musician Danny Keogh. They had two children together, Danielle Riley and Benjamin Storm. In April 1994 Presley announced she and Keogh were separating, on amicable terms. (They have remained very good friends since). She flew to the Dominican Republic to obtain a "quickie" divorce, which was finalised on May 6. Just 20 days later, she married Michael Jackson.

The unlikely pair had first met in 1975 when the

BELOW: Fans of the superstar couple followed their every move on their visit to Hungary.

Michael Jackson meets
the legendary mime artist
Marcel Marceau.

young Lisa-Marie was taken to see some Jacksons concerts in Las Vegas. When they came back into contact, "things moved very quickly". They spoke daily and Jackson proposed over the phone. Elizabeth Taylor has been reported as saying that Michael told her he was in love with Lisa-Marie and was going to marry her even before this. "He needs me," Lisa-Marie, heiress to a huge estate, is said to have asserted. "Someone young and vibrant, like he is. Like Michael, my future is ahead of me. His is ahead of him."

She was in Vegas at the same time as Michael was filming *Jackson Family Honors* at the MGM Grand Garden. Michael asked her out, to a Temptations concert, in February 1994. They were seen holding hands. Later Lisa-Marie and her children spent time at Neverland. "One of the things that most attracted

me to Lisa is that she gets along swell with the animals in my zoo," said Michael. Donald Trump said, "They looked like any other lovey-dovey couple to me." Others claimed, "She was out of her mind for this guy. Maybe it's hard to believe for some, but true, just the same." Michael is said to have pursued her with gifts and flowers. They married in La Vega, a tiny Dominican village. If it was a publicity stunt, it's odd that the media didn't find out about it until several weeks afterwards. The pair honeymooned at the Casa De Campo resort. Asked about early rumours by a newsman, Liz Taylor said, "That's the most ridiculous thing I've ever heard. Michael Jackson is a sane and reasonable man. He's not crazy!" The newly-weds visited Disney World. Lisa-Marie later observed, "Elvis liked to wear uniforms. So does Michael. Elvis loved amusement parks.

Michael has his own amusement park." When the news broke worldwide, she said she was very much in love and they'd kept it secret to prevent a "happy occasion" becoming a "media circus". But now the circus was in town, as headlines shrieked of "the odd couple marriage of the century".

With the charges against Michael rearing their ugly head, some journalists theorized that Michael was now manipulating his way not just to a "testosterone image boost" but a greater stake in the Elvis song catalogue to match his Beatles copyrights. Michael told conflicting versions of the proposal story, saying he'd handed her a diamond ring in the living room at Neverland after the pair had watched the movie *All About Eve*. "We both love that movie," he added. As the period grew more trying for Jackson, Lisa-Marie gave emotional support. She expressed concern over his health and his fondness for prescription drugs. "I believed he didn't do anything wrong," she said, "and that he was wrongly accused. And I started falling for him. I wanted to save him. I felt I could do it." She was instrumental in persuading him to settle out of court with the Chandlers, and to get help with rehabilitation regarding his medication. When in 2009 he died, she released a statement saying she felt that she had in some way "failed" to save him from the "inevitable". "A loss on so many levels," she put it.

In 1995 the authenticity of their romance was, they hoped, proven by their appearance together in the video for Michael's latest single "You Are Not Alone". It was a very public display of affection. As they smooched across a lavender-and-pink backdrop, Lisa-Marie wore nothing but a towel around her waist, Michael little more. In September 1994 the pair had pre-empted this at the 11th Annual MTV Video Music Awards, their first night out under the lights together as man and wife, at Radio City Music Hall in New York. They kissed lengthily in front of millions of TV viewers. And in June 1995 – tieing in with the release of Michael's next album, *HIStory* – they were interviewed together by Diane Sawyer on her ABC show *Prime Time Live*. They spoke of their youthful meetings and recent reunion, of how they might move to Switzerland and have kids together. Lisa-Marie scoffed at suggestions that their marriage was a convenient sham. "Why would I marry somebody I didn't love? I admire and respect him, and I love

him." Unfortunately for Michael, he snapped of the Chandler allegations, "That whole thing is a lie", thus breaching the confidentiality settlement, and the Chandlers initiated fresh proceedings. (These were, again, settled privately). As if to change the subject, Lisa-Marie faced Sawyer brazenly and said, "Do we have sex? Go ahead. Is that what you were going to ask? Yes, yes, yes!"

Soon though, she and her children were holidaying with ex-husband Danny Keogh in Hawaii, and the fairytale was all but over. When Michael fell ill rehearsing for an HBO TV special, *One Night Only,* Lisa-Marie visited him in hospital, but they discussed divorce terms. A lot of money went Lisa-Marie's way, plus a percentage of the royalties on *HIStory*. In return she agreed never to release any kind of "kiss-and-tell" book. The divorce came through on January 18, 1996 in LA. Presley dropped the "Jackson" from her name. She grew close to Janet Jackson for a spell afterwards, but on later rare meetings with Michael emphasised they were "strictly friends". (In 2005 she was considered as a witness for Jackson's trial, and released a statement saying she never saw "improper behaviour".) In 2002 she married the actor Nicolas Cage, a keen Elvis fan. He filed for divorce just 108 days later. In 2006, now a recording artist herself, she married for a fourth time, in Japan, to producer/guitarist Michael Lockwood. Danny Keogh was best man.

Strangely, it wasn't long before Michael, too, was married again. He was to marry nurse Debbie Rowe in 1996 and the couple were to have two children. Before looking to his future though, he was making *HIStory*. Or to give it its full title, *HIStory: Past, Present And Future – Book One*. This was a double album, a greatest hits collection with a bonus disc of new material, released in June 1995. The new songs included some of his most memorable, such as "You Are Not Alone" (with the aforementioned Lisa-Marie video), "Scream" and "Earth Song". There was also his cover of The Beatles' "Come Together", first recorded during the *Bad* sessions. This was Michaels's first official compilation, though several were to follow. "Scream" led to the most expensive video ever made, and perhaps gave the most valid insight available into Jackson's tortured state of mind during this arduous period.

BLOOD ON THE DANCEFLOOR

HIStory was another commercial giant, selling 20 million copies despite Jackson's recent highly-publicised troubles. Michael himself was disappointed by the figures, but may have had to entertain an uncharacteristic whisk of realism. It wasn't as if nobody already owned his hits. While clearly no record, by any artist, was going to match the peak sales of *Thriller*, the new release's more-than-respectable sales proved he could still "cut it" aged 40.

HIStory Begins featured the likes of "Billie Jean", "Bad" and other generation-defining hotspots. *HIStory Continues* offered the new songs. "I believe in perfection," he said. "I try to create that in everything we do. I believe in perfect execution and when we don't get at least 99.9%, I get really upset." Songs like "Tabloid Junkie" and "Smile" gave contrasting glimpses into Michael's psyche. He showed off his musicianship too, playing (for the first time on an album) keyboards, synthesisers, guitars and percussion. The first single from the double album was "Scream", a stunning slice of controlled anger, and a duet with his sister Janet, by now a superstar in her own right. She felt she'd proven she could hack it as a solo singer, and was no longer worried that people would accuse her of "riding on Michael's coat-tails". Indeed her charisma in the video is every bit as electric as her brother's. Said video was, at $5 million dollars, the most expensive ever made. A striking whirl of monochrome sci-fi-influenced imagery featuring extrovert, confessional, sexually charged gesturing from both Jacksons, it's one of the best in their entire body of work. It won three MTV Awards and a Grammy for Best Music Video. The song struggled to contain Michael's fury at the tabloid press and the exaggerations and repetitions of falsehoods which haunted him so. "Stop pressuring me!" begs and commands its refrain.

"You Are Not Alone", the next single, was noted for Lisa-Marie's near-naked video performance (with Michael equally disrobed), and sold three million copies across the world. It was also the first song ever to debut at number one on the *Billboard* chart, its publicity campaign undeniably boosted by the Jackson-Presley union. There followed "Earth Song", another million-seller and an enormous Christmas hit in the UK. It was his biggest British hit. Its video, a masterpiece of excess, found Michael in Messianic pose as he pleaded the case for environmentalism and advocated looking after the planet for our children's children's sake. Its message may not have been subtle, but, like so many Jackson songs, it transcended barriers of language, culture and geography, and was effective all across the planet of its title. The catchy "They Don't Care About Us", on the other hand, provoked controversy, drawing protests from the Anti-Defamation League who saw it as "anti-Semitic". Michael apologised, changing the lyrics and asserting

Legends and performances: (**LEFT**) Michael Jackson and his trademark trilby hat on stage; (**RIGHT**) an epic live rendition of "Earth Song"; and (**BELOW**) meeting Nelson Mandela in South Africa.

that "the song was intended to fight prejudice".

The subsequent world tour, designed to reaffirm his status as the King of Pop and defy those who said his star was on the wane, took in 82 concerts in 58 cities, playing to almost five million fans. The promotional blitz beforehand, for tour and album, was perhaps his most intense and eye-catching yet. A video was released portraying Jackson marching at the tip of several thousand soldiers and military personnel amid explosions and helicopters as children screamed and girls swooned. In Europe, Sony organized for giant statue-like casts of Michael to be floated down major rivers in big cities. One such effigy, 40 feet tall, sailed down the Thames in London, astride a boat. The tour commenced in Prague on September 7, 1996 and closed in Durban, South Africa on October 25, 1997. In South Africa, Lisa-Marie visited him, suggesting, "All is forgiven".

In *Melody Maker*, my own response to Jackson's Wembley stadium show of July 26, 1997, as mentioned in this book's introduction, was one of giddy euphoria. I argued that some "astonishingly sour, curdled reviews" of the tour "betrayed pop". "Of course he thinks he's God," the piece continued, "that's the whole point. Stellar leaps of faith. He's had a rough few years, but immortals can handle the brief candle of scandal." The review closed, "You drew breath in the same century as Michael Jackson. That's entertainment. Be very grateful." As time went by, it grew harder to believe without qualification.

As if the tour wasn't eventful enough, Michael married for the second time during its Australian leg in 1996. Madonna wasn't alone in exclaiming,

"Who the hell is Debbie Rowe?" Surprising even the most diligent of Jackson-watchers, he and the dermatologist nurse Rowe had two children. "I would never do this for money," said Rowe in response to the usual sceptical coverage. "I did this because I love him. That's the only reason I did this." Their son Michael Joseph Jackson Jr,'s name was changed, after their divorce, to Prince Michael Jackson. Their daughter, born in 1998, was named Paris Michael

LEFT: Michael plays the part on the set while making the video for "Scream".

RIGHT: An altogether calmer Michael before the camera in a 1995 shoot.

Katherine Jackson. Jackson had first met Rowe during the previous decade, after he'd been diagnosed with the skin disorder vitiligo. She had treated him since, across the world, and the couple had grown close. When she first became pregnant, Jackson's mother Katherine encouraged them to marry. "My friendship with him is the most important thing to me, and if this marriage gets in the way of that friendship, then we'll put the marriage aside," Rowe said. The wedding took place in the star's suite at the Sheraton On The Park Hotel in Sydney. He gave her a two-and-a-half carat diamond, set into platinum.

This being Jackson, the unorthodox was inevitable,

as was an unwise blast of candour. He confessed that after Paris's birth in Beverly Hills he was in such an excitable state that he tried to leave the hospital with her and take her home, covered in blood, wrapped in a blanket, the minute she was born, taking the placenta along with him. "I am on top of the world," Rowe maintained. The children were generally shielded from view, sometimes even veiled or masked. This again led to much questioning of Jackson's parenting skills. After the 1999 divorce Rowe agreed to give full custody of the children to the singer.

Another album came out in 1997. *Blood On The Dancefloor (HIStory In The Mix)* was a collection of

LEFT: Happy family: Michael and Debbie Rowe with their two children, Michael Joseph Jackson Jr and Paris Michael Katherine Jackson.

RIGHT: Michael's legendary half-time performance during Superbowl XXVII in Pasadena.

eight remixes of hits from *HIStory* added to five new songs. With global sales of over six million, it was the best selling remix album ever. Although it barely broke the top 20 in the US, it was certified platinum. It topped the British charts, as did the single release of the excellent Teddy Riley-produced title track, a slinky, foxy return to form and the last UK number one of his lifetime. In *Uncut* magazine, I reviewed the album. While sniffing at the "hybrid marketing concept, which makes it less of an event, thus shooting our generation's cross between Fred Astaire and *Moby Dick* in the blowhole," I sang the praises of three of the new tracks. "Blood On The Dancefloor" was "his best single in aeons: it kicks, crackles and spits, and rediscovers the narcissistic sass which launched him... is there mileage in Michael still? There is. This record's better side shows there are as many tigers in his tank as bats in his belfry." "Ghosts" and "Is It Scary" were "staccato and compulsive... he's a possessed, pulsatile nu-soul singer." "Morphine" (now there's a title) was "striking, incongruous, and rocks", while "Superfly Sister" was less effective. "Overall, it's amazing how un-seriously we sometimes take him."

According to *Forbes*, Jackson earned $35 million in 1996 and another $20 million in 1997. But he had serious overheads that were to come back to bite. Tangentially, his parents, Joe and Katherine Jackson, had filed for bankruptcy in March 1999. Michael engaged a new manager, Prince Alwaleed, a member of the Saudi royal family, and together they built up Kingdom Entertainment, which developed interests in theme parks, hotels and restaurants and movie projects. His charity work continued, gaining real traction towards the close of the Nineties. The "Michael Jackson And Friends" benefit shows in Germany and Korea raised huge sums, and he played a charity concert in Modena in Italy with Luciano Pavarotti for War Child, in aid of the Kosovan refugees. He also raised big money for the Red Cross, UNESCO and the Nelson Mandela Children's Fund. His reputation was, to a fair degree, being restored. In 2000 he made the *Guinness Book of Records* for supporting 39 charities, more than any other celebrity. As Michael Jackson, the applauded if mercurial philanthropist, entered the 21st century, he must have felt he had weathered a storm, got through the bad times. He was a father. And he had hope.

CRY

It wasn't to be his happiest century. His 2001 comeback
album, titled, with typical bravado, *Invincible* – his first
full studio album since *Dangerous*, a decade earlier – went
double platinum and sold eight million copies. Only by
Michael Jackson's standards could this be deemed a flop,
but the media hungrily labelled it that. Jackson, shooting
himself in the good foot, became embroiled in a heated
dispute with Sony, which certainly didn't help. The record
had cost a reported $30 million to make. Jackson argued
with Sony head Tommy Mottola over the promotional
campaign. He claimed that the company had demanded a
six-figure sum "to pay them back for marketing costs". Sony
protested that on the contrary, they had laid out huge sums
on a "disappointing" project. Jackson then accused Mottola
of racism, saying that if he was white the label would have
done more for his album. This attack astonished even his
own circle, with only his brothers supporting him on the
sensitive issue. But even the Rev. Al Sharpton, approached
for help by Jackson, admitted that Mottola "has always been
supportive of the black music industry." "Music moguls are
liars," raged Jackson, "they manipulate history. If you go
to the record store on the corner, you won't see one black
face. You'll see Elvis Presley and the Rolling Stones. The
attack on me began after I broke Elvis' sales and The Beatles'
sales. It's a conspiracy. I was called a freak, a homosexual
and a child molester." He accused Mottola, who had been
married to Mariah Carey, of being a "devil". Sony retorted
that Jackson's remarks were "ludicrous, spiteful and
hurtful." A year later, Mottola was no longer head of Sony,
and disagreements continue as to whether this was related.
Jackson and Sony also separated on bad terms.

As Michael flew to New York in March 2001 to be inducted into the Rock'n'Roll Hall Of Fame, the youngest person ever to receive the honour, he said, "I'd rather receive praise from my fans than think about the people on my enemy list." Later that month, by means of habitually bizarre contrast, he appeared at the Oxford Union at Oxford University (England) to help launch the charity Heal The Kids, and broke into tears in front of his audience. He spoke of his lost youth: "I wanted to be a typical little boy... but my father had it otherwise and all I could do was envy the laughter and playtime that seemed to be going on all around me." He then said he felt "the weight of my past lifted from my shoulders." "All of us are a product of our childhoods," he told the Oxford audience. "But I am the product of a lack of childhood. If you don't have the memory of being loved, you are condemned to search the world for something to fill you up."

Almost as consolation, *Invincible*, released with five different coloured sleeves, yielded hits like "You Rock My World" (which featured Chris Tucker in the video and Jay-Z on the remix), "Butterflies", "Cry" and "Unbreakable" (with Biggie Smalls). Yet the editor of *Blender* magazine suggested, "I don't think he has earning potential on the music side any more. He has it on the TV side, the rubber-necking freak show side. People will tune in to watch him do anything, but they don't buy his records any more. It's almost impossible to hear his records and not conjure up that scary, weird guy." Michael, undaunted, organized his own promotional extravaganza, to celebrate 30 years as a solo star. Two concerts at Madison Square Garden in New York on September 7 and 10 sold out swiftly, and when shown on CBS TV in November became the channel's highest-rating music special ever, pulling an audience of 40 million viewers. His all-star guests included Whitney Houston, Usher, Ray Charles, Slash, Justin Timberlake and N' Sync, Ricky Martin, Gloria Estefan, Destiny's Child, Liza Minnelli, Dionne Warwick and Luther Vandross. Britney Spears also appeared, duetting with Michael on "The Way You Make Me Feel", but this clip was cut from the TV broadcast, which didn't best please Britney. Michael had also asked legendary actor and on-off friend Marlon Brando to speak at the event, although some reports stated he was enticed by a million-dollar fee. The 77-year-old Brando – one icon who could always give Jackson a

LEFT ABOVE AND BELOW: Michael appears with Justin Timberlake (above) and Britney Spears (below) during his 30th anniversary celebrations in Madison Square Gardens.

RIGHT: Man in the mirror shades in 2005.

run for his money in terms of eccentricity – gave a rambling speech that had some of the crowd booing. He too was edited from the TV show. After Brando however, came the show's true high spot. Michael and his brothers reunited onstage for the first time since 1984 and gave a thrilling medley of greatest hits like "ABC", "I Want You Back", "The Love You Save" and "Can You Feel It".

The joy their performance bred was short-lived. America's emotions were sent reeling by the terrorist attacks of September 11. It was reported that as soon as transport was allowed to move in and out of Manhattan, Michael took Marlon Brando and Elizabeth Taylor to a "secure location" in New Jersey, and that it was left to Janet Jackson to arrange for

the rest of the family to be driven out to California. However Michael soon arranged a benefit concert for the victims of 9/11 at the RFK Stadium in Washington D.C., giving it the name United We Stand: What More Can I Give?

Soon he was revealing another astonishing twist in his own incredible story. Some claim he first broke the news to Marlon Brando, in a limo on the way back from an acting lesson Brando had given in LA. Michael Jackson was about to become a father for the third time. He presented the child, a boy, to the world in February 2002, and to this day the manner of the child's conception is swaddled in mystery. Jackson declared, "I had a personal relationship with the mother," he also confessed that Prince Michael II was

ABOVE: Another rewarding evening: Michael at the Bambi Awards in Germany.

LEFT: Michael was devilishly serious in his protest against Sony's Tommy Mottola.

ABOVE RIGHT: Michael appears in court, accused of backing out of two shows.

the result of artificial insemination. Later he amended his explanation, saying that his own sperm cells had been used with a surrogate mother, whose identity he didn't know. On another occasion he said she was black. As if this wasn't enough strangeness, the baby was to be known as "Blanket". In November, the baby was on the news across the world when cameras caught Jackson dangling him over the outside railings of his hotel suite balcony in Berlin. Fans watched aghast as the baby, wrapped in white cloth, was held precariously with one arm and seemed for a moment to be suspended in mid-air, 50 feet up. As if suddenly realizing the thoughtlessness of his actions, intended to show the infant to the fans, Jackson hauled the boy to safety, narrowly averting tragedy. In response to wide-ranging criticism, he told the press, "I got caught up in the excitement of the moment. I would never intentionally endanger the lives of my children." His unlikely psychic friend Uri Geller defended him by theorising that Michael hadn't been holding the real child but a plastic doll. The whole debacle was just the kind of PR nightmare Michael needed to avoid. The *Independent On Sunday* proposed, "The last decade of Michael Jackson's life has hardly been the most glorious phase of his career, but the events of the last six months have seen him slide downwards at unprecedented speed. If Jackson was ever the "King of Pop", there seems little doubt that his crown has now been broken into small pieces."

There was talk of Michael writing children's books and a sequel to *Moonwalk* to "set the record straight", but nothing came of these proposals. And as a further blow in 2002, the State of California cut the Heal the World Foundation from its tax-exempt status, for not filing annual statements. On a less stressful note, feasibly, Michael and Tito Jackson served as best men at the wedding of Liza Minnelli and David Gest. Elizabeth Taylor was matron of honour. Singers at the reception included Whitney Houston and Tony Bennett. But the period held yet further indignities. *Forbes* called Michael's career "a franchise in demise" and *People* named him "biggest loser of the year". *Vanity Fair* ran a piece suggesting he had tried to set a "voodoo curse" on former friends Spielberg and Geffen. Concert promoter Marcel Avram sued him over cancelled shows. Then at the MTV Annual Video Music Awards in August, Britney Spears, about to present Michael with a birthday cake onstage, spontaneously used the phrase "artist of the

millennium". Michael, misunderstanding, made an acceptance speech where he thanked everybody for honouring him as just that. As the press guffawed, MTV stated that they'd "merely wanted to wish him happy birthday". Some gift.

The next years were to get even worse for the suffering star. The body blow arrived. On February 6, 2003, ITV in the UK and then ABC in the US (who paid the Brits $5 million for the privilege) ran a two-hour, British-produced documentary. Friend Uri Geller had introduced Michael to interviewer Martin Bashir, an ambitious UK journalist who'd acquired fame on the back of a revealing Princess Diana interview. Unwisely, not to say inexplicably, given his decades of tight control over his image, Jackson granted Bashir and his crew "unfettered access" to much of his private life at Neverland for several months. The programme, *Living With Michael Jackson*, showed the singer admitting he had "sleepovers" with young boys. "Why can't you share your bed?" he said to a stunned interviewer. "That's the most loving thing to do, to share your bed with someone." The cringe-inducing scenes continued. Jackson said the sight of his father made him "regurgitate" whenever he saw him, and then, with perhaps a lesser degree of full disclosure, claimed he'd only ever had two operations

on his nose (to help his breathing and singing). Jackson was also shown spending outrageous amounts on shopping sprees. The programme's other disturbing spells included one where a 12-year-old cancer survivor, Gavin Arvizo, cuddled Jackson, speaking of many a night spent in his bed. When Jackson said, "I'm Peter Pan," as if that explained everything, Bashir countered flatly, "You're Michael Jackson." "I'm Peter Pan in my heart," said the star.

Jackson immediately filed complaints, suggesting the editing deliberately portrayed him badly. The fall-out was unstoppable. Stories suggesting child abuse again appeared everywhere, and in 2003 he was arrested on suspicion of molesting Gavin Arvizo. Jackson posted three million dollars bail. The case took until 2005 to come to trial, after one of the most frenzied media circuses of modern times. Jackson sometimes did not help matters, naively showboating to loyal fans outside the courtroom. His Santa Barbara County jail mugshot graced every newspaper. After four months in court, and extensive legal costs, Jackson, pleading not guilty, was acquitted of all charges.

To say that considerable damage was nonetheless done to his reputation and career would be an understatement. His morale may have been shattered from this point on. The fate of a greatest hits compilation, *Number Ones*, paled in significance next to the scandal. (To pour on further awkwardness, the one new track here, "One More Chance", was written by R. Kelly, who in 2002 was himself arrested on 21 counts of child pornography. He too was later acquitted). Jackson's home was trashed by investigators, Neverland despoiled, his body probed, his pride torn down. His financial woes multiplied: it was announced that he owed $200 million in loans, and the promoter Avram won a multi-million dollar payout. An accountant testified that the singer had been spending $30 million per year above what he was earning. Tabloids reported that Michael Jackson had skin cancer.

Although acquitted, the cost to Jackson's fragile psyche was, surely, incalculable. He was eventually forced to sell off stakes in Neverland. In many eyes a pariah in America, he took to a peripatetic, nomadic lifestyle, frequently moving from place to place. He took his children to Bahrain, as the guests of the ruler's son, a friend of Jermaine's. Even this turned sour: the sheik sued him for reneging on a book and

music contract (settling out of court). Some canny leveraging of principal assets kept him afloat. In early 2009 Sony retained an option to buy half his stake in the Sony/ATV catalogue, which includes the Beatles songs, if he defaulted on loans.

"Michael hasn't been back to Neverland since the trial," said La Toya Jackson. "He never wants to see it again. The memories now are so awful." Neverland fell into disrepair. It was 2006 before he made public appearances again, showing up at the *Guinness World Records* office in London to receive eight awards. As well as anniversary reissues of his biggest albums (such as *Thriller 25*), further hits compilations emerged – 2005's *The Essential* and 2008's *King Of Pop*. In the US he joined a crowd of 9,000 to pay his respects at "the godfather of soul" James Brown's funeral. He exchanged hugs with the Rev. Al Sharpton and the Rev. Jesse Jackson. "When I saw James Brown move when I was a small child", he said, "I was mesmerized. Right then and there, I knew that was exactly what I wanted to do for the rest of my life."

He needed a comeback of Lazarus-like proportions. It wasn't the World Music Awards of 2006 in London, where his first stage appearance

ABOVE LEFT: Michael and friends: with Elizabeth Taylor and Macaulay Culkin.

ABOVE: Golden days at Neverland, when the ranch was busy with many visitors.

BELOW LEFT: The Jackson family go trick-or-treating.

since his trial was highly anticipated. He arrived two hours late, sang two verses of "We Are The World", blew kisses, then looked as bewildered as anyone when the music stopped. Fans had been told to expect "Thriller" and more. Beyonce told press she'd had to coax him into even leaving his dressing room. "He didn't want to come out," she said. There was talk – fruitless – of Vegas shows. And then, as whispers that he was finished and washed up turned to murmurs which became rumblings, there came, in March 2009, news to gladden the heart of every loyal, long-suffering, faith-keeping Michael Jackson fan.

This was going to be it.

"THIS IS IT" – THE FINAL CURTAIN CALL

Many had suggested that Michael Jackson's star was all but extinguished. They were to be loudly proven wrong on March 5, 2009. There were scenes of pandemonium and hysteria as seven thousand fans (and 350 reporters) – interestingly, of all ages – reached a feverish level of excitement at London's O2 Arena. They were waiting to hear a very special announcement. After – naturally – keeping everybody waiting, Jackson took the stage 90 minutes late and revealed that a season of live shows – his first since the 1996–97 tour – was to happen. He hadn't played a full concert for eight years.

"This is it. I just want to say these will be my final show performances in London," he said. "When I say this is it, I really mean: this is it. I'll be performing the songs my fans want to hear. This is really it, the final curtain call. I love you, I really do. You have to know that, from the bottom of my heart. This is it – and I'll see you in July."

The shows were due to start on July 9. Initially ten were mooted, but demand was so high that tickets were selling out at a rate of 11 per second. The number of shows was eventually increased to 50, spanning half of 2009 and the first months of 2010. The run would smash Prince's record of 21 nights at the arena. "People will come from all over the world!" exclaimed one TV pundit. "Forget the recession, this could kick-start London's economy!" The promoters, AEG, stated that this would be "history in the making as King of Pop Michael Jackson performs in London for the last time. Long may he reign!" There was even talk of a world tour to follow, one that might earn him as much as $400 million.

Already, some were voicing their doubts about the star's ability to carry off such an extended season. They even asked if the "Michael Jackson" clad in red at the press conference had been an imposter. They questioned his health, energy, fitness, desire. They questioned the thin 50-year-old man's

LEFT: The star announces his huge run of London shows by saying 'This is it!'

ABOVE: Rehearsing for the shows was in full swing in the early summer of 2009.

ability to last 50 gruelling performances. The promoters said that Jackson was "in tremendous condition, after a battery of tests." Supporters willed him to restore his shaken reputation and polish his tarnished crown. Tickets were soon being touted online for thousands of dollars. The comeback was a universal talking point. It was set up to be a spectacle which those fortunate enough to witness would never forget. With one dramatic decision, it seemed he had dissolved all the derision and suspicion and proven once again he was the world's most popular entertainer.

Jackson was photographed house-hunting in the UK with his children. He began a training regime in LA and extensive rehearsals were soon underway at the Staples Centre. Then came the first hint of trouble. The first few sold-out shows were pushed back to July 13, with perfectionism and stage logistics being offered up as reasons. Still, fans remained optimistic. On June 25, their hopes were cruelly crushed.

NEVER CAN
SAY GOODBYE

On Thursday June 25, 2009, Michael Jackson died after suffering
a heart attack at his rented home in Holmby Hills, off Sunset
Boulevard, in Los Angeles. He was reported to have collapsed
and stopped breathing after injections of Demerol, a powerful
painkiller. A call was placed to emergency services at around
12.26p.m. local time. Paramedics tried desperately to revive him,
to no avail. He was taken by ambulance to the nearby UCLA
Medical Centre, where further attempts were made to resuscitate
him. An entourage of around ten people were said to have been
shouting, "You've got to save him!" His mother, various family
members and Elizabeth Taylor rushed to the hospital. Distraught
fans soon began to gather outside and around his home. As news
stations hesitated to accept the truth of the rumours spreading like
wildfire, Los Angeles County Coroner Fred Corral confirmed that
Jackson had died of heart failure at 2.26p.m.

As the planet grieved or gawped, from Gotham to Glastonbury, Jackson's "strange and brilliant" life was eulogized across the planet. News channels and print media dealt with little else. It was, as they say, a good day to bury (other) bad news. "The day the music died," sobbed one fan to camera. In death just as in life, coverage veered manically between celebration (his videos and songs were placed on 24-hour rotation) and ghoulish dissection. Every news programme found a new bone to pick at. The speculation flailed. What was the role of his doctor? What drugs had the star been taking? Had his death been avoidable? As the Jackson family asked for a second autopsy, conspiracy theorists had a field day. Some ghouls went so far as to suggest the death had been faked as a career move, or as a means of avoiding the upcoming live shows. Within days the reliable *National Enquirer* ran a picture of "Jacko Alive", claiming a lookalike had instead died.

But the harrowing truth sank in. The King of Pop was dead. In an atmosphere of near-hysteria, critics queued up to proclaim his genius, to praise, as *Time* magazine put it, "the way he blended black music and white." His "gentleness" was often mentioned. The more analytical and objective discussed on air his "subdivisions", the gap between the artist and the celebrity, the "Frankenstein's monster" his mishaps in the world of plastic surgery had created. It seemed agreed upon that his life and career – still inseparable – had split into three main phases: the youthful innocent of the Jackson 5 days, the thrilling solo superstar of the 80s, and then Wacko Jacko ("a victim of his own hype, in freefall"). "What we are mourning," mused one critic, "is our own memories."

"Even if he had succeeded in making it back to the top for a while," mused Richard Lacayo in *Time*, "it would however always have been difficult to imagine

PREVIOUS PAGE:
Michael's memorial wall
outside the Staples Center
in Los Angeles.

LEFT: Fans gather at the
foot of Paris's Eiffel Tower.

ABOVE: The Los Angeles
Theater pays tribute.

RIGHT: Fans light candles
to their hero outside the
hospital in which he died.

Jackson, the eternal child, in old age." He pictured him becoming ever more reclusive and frightened, like "Gloria Swanson in *Sunset Boulevard*." Happier, and perhaps easier and more comforting, to remember Michael Jackson in his heyday, at the top of his game, his body full of benign fire, his voice somersaulting with ecstasy. It seems probable that posterity will immortalize that performer, once the vultures have worn out their claws on the last chapter in Jackson's own rewriting of *Hollywood Babylon*.

"This is such a tragic loss and a terrible day," said Beyonce Knowles. "Michael Jackson has made a bigger impact than any other artist in the history of music. He was magic. He was what we all strive to be. He will always be the King of Pop." Cher said, "God gives you certain gifts, and this was just an extraordinary child touched by ability. He could sing like nobody else." "I was so excited to see his tour in London," said Britney Spears. "I was going to fly in to see him. He's been an inspiration throughout my entire life and I'm devastated that he's gone." Madonna gave us, "I can't stop crying over the sad news. The world has lost one of its greats, but his music will live on forever." "I'll always cherish the moments I shared with him onstage and all the things I learned about music from him," said Justin Timberlake. Perhaps ex-wife Lisa-Marie Presley's tribute was the most

LEFT: Laying flowers at Michael's star on the Hollywood Walk of Fame.

RIGHT: The golden casket at Michael's memorial service.

BELOW: Jermaine Jackson performs during the memorial service to his brother at the Staples Center.

touching. "I am so very sad and confused with every emotion possible," she announced. "I am heartbroken for his children, who I know were everything to him, and for his family. This is such a massive loss on so many levels. Words fail me."

Words did not fail the media, who continued to run lurid reports of drug abuse, debts and other depressants. When Jackson's will left his estate to his mother and children, and asked for Katherine Jackson (but not his father) to be his children's guardian, with his back-up choice being Diana Ross, they stirred up stories of Debbie Rowe's reaction. They posed puzzlers as to whether Jackson was the children's real father. Then they reported that Michael would be buried at Neverland, before accepting that the state laws of California prevented that.

When this book was first published, there was still much confusion and conjecture. One paper even suggested a hologram of Michael could fulfil the live dates. The recordings in the vaults prompted much speculation. As many as 200 tracks sat unreleased, some said, and while some reports claimed many of these were children's songs, others revealed that Jackson had worked on uncompleted material with contemporary hip-hop/R&B and pop movers and shakers like will.i.am, Akon and Ne-Yo. In 2007 Michael had told *Ebony* magazine, "I'm writing a lot of stuff right now. I'm in the studio every day." Kanye West, T-Pain, Swiss Beatz and Sean Garrett all confirmed they'd met with Jackson to discuss working together. 50 Cent and Chris Brown had both had phone conversations with him about possible projects. And Jackson's collaboration with Akon, "Hold My Hand", leaked online. After working on a remix of "Wanna Be Startin' Somethin'" in 2008, Akon said, "He's a genius. That aura… is incredible. We're about to shake the world up, man! Some artists think regional, some think national, I was thinking international. He thinks planets. It's on another level." Chimed will.i.am,

"I'm a fan of the dude. He's the smartest dude I ever met. You got your Michael Jacksons, your James Browns, Princes, Nat King Coles, just to shed light on the Earth. And he told me what Rock'n'Roll means – it means sex. He is real proud of being black … in the media a lot of the time he's repressed, so you don't always get that."

Poignantly, the song "Hold My Hand" begins, "This life don't last forever..." It goes on, "When it gets dark and when it gets cold/ We can just hold each other till we see the sunlight". Producer Giorgio Tuinfort claims, "He heard my work with Akon and loved it. There were a lot of songs nearly finished, hundreds of demos and two completely finished and ready to go. I have them at home." He adds that he'll leave it to Jackson's family to decide whether they will be released. Epic Records president Amanda Ghost has said there will be no indecent haste. "We just want to pay our respects to Michael. We don't want to be seen to be jumping on any bandwagon associated with his death."

The Jackson family were in full view on the day of Michael Jackson's memorial service. Albeit wearing dark sunglasses and, in the brothers' case, one diamante glove each (in honour of Michael's trademark in happier days). After much rumour and counter-rumour, July 7 saw the family, very publicly united again, beginning the day with a private 40-minute farewell to their brightest star at the Forest Lawn memorial park. They then carried Michael's gold casket, decked with red roses, by motorcade to the Staples Center, where the rest was pure Hollywood, pure showbiz. This was where Michael had been rehearsing, such a brief time ago. Now it became the focus of a reported 31.3 million live TV viewers in America and countless more around the world. As well as 17,500 fans inside the arena, who'd won tickets on an internet lottery, 50,000 more fans had travelled just to stand outside, to say they were there. Part funeral, part tribute concert, part celebration, part royal wake, the event was as over-the-top as we wanted it to be. Jackson's coffin was placed at the front of the stage, the family sitting front row. The *Guardian* could not resist calling it "his final performance... as flawless and precise as his teenaged singing or his legendary dancing in the 80s." It was as moving as only great pomp and unabashed melodrama can be. The eulogies were rose-tinted, the singers' voices cracked with emotion both genuine and professional. One recalled that Michael had once said that he hoped his funeral would be the greatest show on Earth.

Smokey Robinson read messages from Nelson Mandela and Diana Ross (Ross, like Elizabeth Taylor

and Quincy Jones, elected to avoid what Taylor called the "hoop-la", preferring to grieve in private). This was to be a very public outpouring of emotion, remembering a great entertainer and forgetting his detractors.

A backdrop showed stills and footage of Michael performing at various stages in his life as Mariah Carey sang "I'll Be There", Lionel Richie sang "Jesus Is Love" and Stevie Wonder sang "Never Dreamed You'd Leave In Summer", changing the ending to "Michael, why didn't you stay?" Berry Gordy Jr. proclaimed Jackson "the greatest entertainer that ever lived," to a standing ovation. Queen Latifah read a specially-written poem by Maya Angelou. "He'll never really be gone," said Smokey. LA Lakers stars past and present Magic Johnson and Kobe Bryant offered fond reminiscences of their friend. Jennifer Hudson sang Michael's song "Will You Be There?" John Mayer played "Human Nature". The tears fell more openly as Jermaine Jackson performed the Charlie Chaplin song, "Smile", which Brooke Shields had introduced as Michael's favourite song. She spoke of their "natural and easy friendship... yes, it may have seemed odd to the outside, but we made it fun and real." She emphasized his sensitivity and love of life. The Rev. Al Sharpton tore up a storm, shouting, "He broke down the color curtain. He put us on the cover of magazines and TV. He made us love each other." He attributed President Obama's election victory and many other things to Michael. "It's not about the mess," he declared, urging America not to think about the scandal-riddled later years, "It's about his message." Climactically he looked at Jackson's children and said, "Wasn't nothing strange about your daddy. What was strange was what your daddy had to deal with." And indeed there were Michael's three children: visible, unveiled, beautiful.

There was more. Usher sang "Gone Too Soon", crying as he touched the coffin. The son and daughter of civil rights leader Martin Luther King gave powerful speeches. Twelve-year-old Welsh schoolboy Shaheen Jafargholi, spotted by Jackson on a British TV talent show, sang "Who's Lovin' You?" "I want to thank him for blessing me and every single individual with his amazing music," he said. It seemed the finale would be massed renditions of "We Are The World" and "Heal The World", as designed for the "This Is It" shows, with the family and friends joining the cast onstage. Yet even after this there were further emotional punches. Marlon Jackson said, "Maybe now, Michael, they will leave you alone." Then, as if to stun Jackson's critics into silence, his children were nudged towards the

RIGHT: Quincy Jones discusses Jackson in Hollywood, January 2012. Cirque du Soleil's Immortal World Tour was a huge success.

BELOW: Michael's friends and family look on as a memorial is unveiled at Jackson's childhood home in Gary, Indiana, in June 2010, the first anniversary of the performer's death.

microphone. "Speak up, honey," said Janet as 11-year-old Paris topped her public debut by addressing the mesmerised watching world. "Ever since I was born," she managed before dissolving into tears, "Daddy has been the best father you could ever imagine, and I just wanted to say I love him so much." Genuinely, almost unbearably moving and disarming, it surpassed Elton John's performance of "Candle In The Wind" at Princess Diana's funeral as an iconic moment in that indefinable, very modern zone which overlaps glamour, tragedy, voyeurism, illusion and the real.

Some called it exploitation. Some called it charisma. Some called it sad, attributing differing meanings to the adjective. At that moment, she was the biggest star in the world. As Michael Jackson had been for most of his 50 frenetic years on Earth.

"From the first time people heard him sing as a young boy," said Berry Gordy, "Michael Jackson went into orbit and never came down."

In the years following Michael's death, his star can still be found very much in ascendance, his music continuing to soundtrack lives everywhere. The first posthumous release from his estate was the song "This Is It", which lent its title to the subsequent blockbuster. Based on an old demo and co-written by Jackson and Paul Anka back in the Eighties, it had the added bonus of backing vocals by the other Jackson brothers, who'd gathered in a studio for the first time in 20 years. It was a teaser for the film Michael Jackson's *This Is It*, released on October 28, 2009.

The spectacular movie – a documentary formed from footage shot during and around rehearsals for the tour that never happened – only ran for a special limited two-week engagement, but swiftly became one of the highest-grossing music documentaries of all time. Worldwide, it took over $260 million (with 90 per cent of profits going to the Jackson estate). The opening weekend alone took in over £100 million at the box office. It also sold well on DVD, reaffirming Jackson's enduring popularity. It was dedicated, after all, to "the fans".

There was a curious mixture of elation and sadness for fans as they watched Jackson honing numbers, songs and dance routines with a brilliantly talented and enthused team. He still "had it" during those rehearsals at The Staples Center and The Forum in California; it was abundantly evident. Director Kenny Ortega confirmed that the footage hadn't originally been intended for general release, but nonetheless the performances crackled with electricity, energy and passion, Sony having edited

down hundreds of hours of film. There were moments of humour too, with Michael's quips and encouragement often putting his star-struck co-performers at ease. Some fans and critics complained that the singer wouldn't have wanted the film shown, as he was such a perfectionist, but in fact it renders the enigmatic star more likeable, showing his eagerness to make the show special and his willingness to work hard. Plus, of course, it showed off his natural, and still breath-taking, ability to perform.

For many, the highlights will live in the memory as vividly as any pinnacles in Michael's long career. His emerging from a "body" made of screens to begin "Wanna Be Startin' Somethin'". The a capella sequences. The choreography, throughout. The intense mix of film and dancing for "Bad" and "Jam"; the wonderful run-throughs of "Human Nature". Green-screen rehearsals of "Smooth Criminal". Jackson and Ortega fine-tuning the steps of the "Thriller" extras. A touching medley of Jackson 5 material, and a heart-breaking rendition of "I Just Can't Stop Loving You" with Judith Hill.

Guitarist Orianthi Panagaris excels on "Black Or White", Michael urging her on with her solos. There's also an outstanding scene in which Michael gamely tries out the "cherry-picker" device designed to carry him above the audience, mid-air. "Earth Song", "Billie Jean" and a climactic "Man In The Mirror" strongly suggest this would have been one of the all-time great shows. If they sound and look this great in soundchecks, we can only imagine how exhilarating they would have been with the stabilizers off. *This Is It* truly was, as the posters claimed, "Michael Jackson like you've never seen him before." Esteemed film critic Roger Ebert hailed the movie as "extraordinary...something else." *The Hollywood Reporter* remarked that the film was "strange, but strangely beguiling" and captured Jackson in "feverish grips of pure creativity". *Rolling Stone* thought it "illuminating, unnerving and unforgettable" and "a transcendent tribute".

A *This Is It* compilation album followed instantly, carrying two versions of the title song along with the many hits in the order in which they appeared in the film,

A Michael Jackson impersonator performs during the *Thriller – Live!* concert at Beijing's Exhibition Theatre in 2010. The show has been popular around the world.

though in their original recorded versions. A bonus disc offered some previously unreleased alternative versions, as well as Michael reciting a poem, "Planet Earth". The album went straight in at number one on the Billboard chart, selling over 373,000 copies in its first seven days. The 2009 American Music Awards saw fit to honour Michael with no less than four posthumous awards.

A year after the tragic events of June 25, 2009, fans in large numbers marked the first anniversary of Jackson's death by visiting his family home and his star on Hollywood's Walk of Fame. Sunflowers were a common tribute, as were red roses. On the thousandth day after his passing, fans placed one thousand roses on the steps at Forest Lawn Cemetery, his resting place. The family too, despite some further unseemly financial wrangling, paid their respects. A granite monument was unveiled outside the old family abode in Gary, Indiana. There was a candlelight vigil by more zealous fans and a performance of "We Are The World". Katherine Jackson published a new book, entitled *Never Can Say Goodbye*, while Jermaine updated his candid and sincere *You Are Not Alone: Michael, Through A Brother's Eyes*. There were, too, interesting and ambitious literary studies of the whole phenomenon, like *The Resistible Demise of Michael Jackson*.

As time has gone by, the tributes continue. These have ranged from the highly eccentric, such as Mohamed Al-Fayed's erection of a controversial statue by Fulham Football Club's Craven Cottage stadium, which was unveiled in April 2011 (and removed by the football club's new owner in September 2013), to the more vibrant, including the long-running London West End musical *Thriller*. There have been dancing-and-singing video games, and a PlayStation release, *Michael Jackson: The Experience*. At the end of 2009, the American Film Institute hailed the star's death as a "moment of significance", praising "the unprecedented global eulogy of his posthumous concert rehearsal movie *This Is It*". The following year, the National Museum of Dance and Hall of Fame also honoured him. He remains the first and only dancer from the pop world to have been inducted.

Record sales continued to soar. In the year after his death, Michael Jackson sold more albums than anybody else, with over 35 million albums bought worldwide. He became the first artist to break the one-million-downloads-in-a-week barrier. Sony, understandably, broke the bank to extend their distribution rights, which were due to run out in 2015, to at least 2017. It's reported they have many albums of material – as many as ten,

perhaps – ready for potential release.

The first of these was simply titled *Michael*. It came out at the end of 2010, led by the single "Breaking News" (which dealt with the media's obsession with pop icons). (A promotional poster at the Rectory Farm in Middlesex, UK was officially the largest poster in the world). This miscellany of unreleased tracks (recorded between 1982 and 2010) received mixed reviews, from "very impressive" to "a hotchpotch". Production credits were shared between a sprawling cast of Jackson, Akon, Lenny Kravitz, Angelikson, Brad Buxer, Theron "Neff-U" Feemster, John McClain, Tricky Stewart, Giorgio Tuinfort and Teddy Riley.

The album's ten tracks included four more new singles, released between November 2010 and July 2011: the aforementioned "Hold My Hand", "Hollywood Tonight", "Behind The Mask" and "(I Like) The Way You Love Me". The track "Best Of Joy" was written and recorded in 2009, and thus stands as one of the last Michael created during his lifetime. Despite outspoken sceptics from Dave Grohl to will.i.am, the *Michael* album, while failing to match the figures of *This Is It*, has gone platinum in 18 countries.

There will be more releases of stockpiled music, certainly, with unfinished tracks being polished for public airing. Yet as well as the taste of the tunes, people still want to feel and recall the matchless live-performer charisma of Jackson. One huge success in this field of keeping-the-flame-burning is Cirque Du Soleil's show *Michael Jackson: The Immortal World Tour*. Launched in Montreal in October 2011, the 90-minute production combines Jackson-esque choreography with the troupe's signature aerial displays and agility. While the tour is proving immensely popular, a larger, more immersive, sibling show called *Michael Jackson: One* opened in residency in May 2013 in Las Vegas. The fans won't stop because they can't get enough. The Jacksons (Jackie, Tito, Marlon, Randy and Jermaine) have toured again, with some of Michael's numbers in their set. Said Jermaine, "This was not, as some tired cynics tried to suggest, an attempt to imitate Michael. That is an impossibility."

At the beginning of his book, Jermaine quotes the Roman poet Horace, who in 23 BC exclaimed: "I shall not totally die, and a great part of me will live beyond Death: I will keep growing, fresh with the praise of posterity." Michael Jackson, the star of stars, who is now embedded in entertainment's Peter Pantheon, continues to shine as brightly as he ever did and will do so, in the hearts and minds of his fans, forever.

RIGHT: Flowers and other tributes placed at the grave of Michael Jackson in Forest Lawn Cemetary, Glendale, California, June 2013.

BELOW: A street tribute to Michael Jackson in Toronto, Canada. One of many impromptu celebrations in the weeks after his death in 2009.

DISCOGRAPHY

SINGLES

JACKSON 5

1968	"Big Boy"/"You've Changed"
	"We Don't Have To Be Over 21"
1969	"I Want You Back"
1970	"ABC"
	"The Love You Save"
	"I'll Be There"
	"Santa Claus Is Coming to Town"
	"I Saw Mommy Kissing Santa Claus"
1971	"Mama's Pearl"
	"Never Can Say Goodbye"
	"Maybe Tomorrow"
	"Sugar Daddy"
	"Little Bitty Pretty One"
1972	"Lookin' Through the Windows"
	"Doctor My Eyes"
	"Corner of the Sky"
1973	"Hallelujah Day"
	"Skywriter"
	"Get It Together"
1974	"The Boogie Man"
	"Dancing Machine"
	"Whatever You Got I Want"
	"Life Of The Party"
	"I Am Love (Part 1)"
1975	"Forever Came Today"
	"All I Do"

THE JACKSONS

1976	"Enjoy Yourself"
1977	"Show You the Way to Go"
	"Dreamer"
	"Goin' Places"
	"Even Though You're Gone"
1978	"Different Kind Of Lady"
	"Music's Taking Over"
	"Find Me a Girl"
	"Blame It on the Boogie"
1979	"Shake Your Body (Down to the Ground)"
	"Destiny"
1980	"Lovely One"
1981	"This Place Hotel"
	"Can You Feel It"
	"Walk Right Now"
	"Time Waits For No One"
	"Things I Do For You"
1984	"State of Shock" (with Mick Jagger)
	"Torture"
	"Body"
	"Wait"

MICHAEL JACKSON

1971	"Got to Be There"
1972	"Rockin' Robin"
	"I Wanna Be Where You Are"
	"Ain't No Sunshine"
	"Ben"
1973	"Music and Me"
	"Happy"
1975	"We're Almost There"
	"Just a Little Bit of You"
1979	"You Can't Win"
	"Don't Stop 'til You Get Enough"
	"Rock with You"
1980	"Off the Wall"
	"She's out of My Life"
	"Girlfriend"
1981	"One Day in Your Life"
1983	"Billie Jean"
	"Beat It"'
	"Wanna Be Startin' Somethin'"
	"Human Nature"
1984	"Thriller"
	"Farewell My Summer Love"
	"Bad"
1988	"The Way You Make Me Feel"
	"Man in the Mirror"
	"Dirty Diana"
	"Another Part of Me"
	"Smooth Criminal"
1989	"Leave Me Alone"
	"Liberian Girl"
1991	"Black or White"
1992	"Remember the Time"
	"In the Closet"
	"Jam"
	"Who Is It"
	"Heal the World"
1993	"Give in to Me"

"Will You Be There"
"Gone Too Soon"
1995   "Scream/Childhood"
"You Are Not Alone"
"Earth Song"
"They Don't Care About Us"
"Stranger in Moscow"
1997   "Blood on the Dance Floor"
"HIStory/Ghosts"
2001   "You Rock My World"
"Cry"
2002   "Butterflies"
"Heaven Can Wait"
2003   "What More Can I Give"
"One More Chance"

COLLABORATIONS

1978   "Ease on Down the Road" (with Diana Ross)
1979   "A Brand New Day" (with Diana Ross)
1980   "Save Me" (with Dave Mason)
1983   "Say Say Say" (with Paul McCartney)
1984   "Somebody's Watching Me" (with Rockwell)
1987   "I Just Can't Stop Loving You"
      (with Siedah Garrett)
1982   "The Girl Is Mine" (with Paul McCartney)
1988   "Get It" (with Stevie Wonder)
1991   "Do the Bartman" (with The Simpsons)
1992   "Whatzupwitu" (with Eddie Murphy)
1996   "This Time Around"
      (with The Notorious B.I.G.)
"Why" (with 3T)
2008   "The Girl Is Mine 2008" (with will.i.am)
"Wanna Be Startin' Somethin'" (with Akon)

ALBUMS

JACKSON 5

1969   *Diana Ross Presents the Jackson 5*
1970   *ABC*
Third Album
The Jackson 5 Christmas Album
1971   *Maybe Tomorrow*
Goin' Back to Indiana
1972   *Lookin' Through the Windows*
1973   *Skywriter*
The Jackson 5 in Japan

G.I.T.: Get It Together
1974   *Dancing Machine*
1975   *Moving Violation*

THE JACKSONS

1976   *The Jacksons*
1977   *Goin' Places*
1978   *Destiny*
1980   *Triumph*
1981   *The Jacksons Live!*
1984   *Victory*

MICHAEL JACKSON

1972   *Got to Be There*
Ben
1973   *Music & Me*
1975   *Forever, Michael*
1979   *Off the Wall*
1982   *Thriller*
1987   *Bad*
1991   *Dangerous*
1995   *HIStory: Past, Present and Future, Book One*
1997   *Blood on the Dance Floor (HIStory in the Mix)*
2001   *Invincible*

2009–2011 RELEASES

Since Michael's passing, the singer's record label has continued to release material. The selected list below accounts for singles and compilation albums.

SINGLES
2010   "Hold My Hand" (with Akon)
2010   "Breaking News"
2010   "I Can't Make It Another Day (with
      Lenny Kravitz)
2010   "Monster" (With 50 Cent)
2011   "I Like The Way You Love Me"
2011   "Hollywood Tonight"
2011   "Behind The Mask"

COMPILATIONS, SELECTED
2009   *Michael Jackson's This Is It*
2009   *Selections from Michael Jackson's
      This Is It*
2010   *Michael*
2011   *Immortal*

PICTURE CREDITS

The publishers would like to thank the following sources for their kind permission to reproduce the pictures in this book.

1. Getty Images/Kevin Mazur; 3. Getty Images/Al Messerschmidt; 4-5. Getty Images/Dave Hogan; 6. Corbis/Str/Reuters; 7. Getty Images/Phil Dent/Redferns; 8. Getty Images/Kevin Mazur/Wireimages; 10. Getty Images/Kevin Mazur/Wireimage; 11. Getty Images/Kevin Winter; 12. Allstar Picture Library; 14. Getty Images/Michael Ochs Archives; 15. Getty Images/Michael Ochs Archives; 16. Rex Features/Fotos International; 17. Getty Images/John Olson/Time & Life Pictures; 18. Press Association Images/Landov: 19. Press Association Images/AP; 21. Getty Images/Michael Ochs Archives; 22. Getty Images/GAB Archive/Redferns; 23. Getty Images/Giles Petard/Redferns; 24. Getty Images/Michael Ochs Archives; 25. Getty Images/Michael Ochs Archives; 26. Getty Images/CBS Photo Archive; 27. Getty Images/Julian Wasser/Time & Life Pictures; 28. Getty Images/Michael Ochs Archives; 29. Retna/Landov (top); 29. Corbis/Steve Schapiro/Outline (bottom); 31. Corbis/Laura Levine; 32. Getty Images/Michael Ochs Archive; 33. Allstar Picture Library (top); 33. Getty Images/Jim McCrary/Redferns (bottom); 34. Getty Images/Ron Galella/Wireimage (top); 34. Getty Images/Michael Ochs Archives (bottom); 35. Getty Images/Michael Ochs Archives; 36. Corbis/Robert Matheu/Retna Ltd.; 37. Corbis/Lynn Goldsmith (top); 37. Corbis/Robert Matheu/Retna Ltd. (bottom); 38. Corbis/Lynn Goldsmith (top); 38. Getty Images/Lester Cohen/Wireimage (bottom); 39. Getty Images/Ebet Roberts/Redferns; 40. Corbis/Lynn Goldsmith (left); 40. Getty Images/Ron Galella/Wireimage (right); 41. Corbis/© Andy Warhol Foundation/© The Andy Warhol Foundation for the Visual Arts; 42-43. Allstar Picture Library; 44. Getty Images/GAB Archive/Redferns; 46. Corbis/Lynn Goldsmith; 47. Getty Images/Chris Walter/Wireimage; 48. Corbis/Walter McBride/Retna Ltd.; 49. Getty Images/Dave Hogan; 50. Getty Images/Time & Life Pictures/DMI; 51. Corbis/Chris Walter/Wireimage; 52. Allstar Picture Library; 53. Corbis/William Snyder/Dallas Morning News; 54. Rex Features; 55. Retna/Landov; 56. Getty Images/Jack Kightlinger/White House/Time & Life Pictures; 57. Getty Images/Ron Galella/Wireimage; 58. Getty Images/Richard E. Aaron/Redferns; 59. Corbis/Bettmann; 60-65. Corbis/Douglas Kirkland; 66. Getty Images/Kevin Mazur/Wireimage; 68. Rex Features/Everett Collection (top); 68. Rex Features/Sipa Press (bottom); 69. Kobal Collection/Ultimate Productions; 70. Corbis/Neal Preston; 71. Corbis/Lori Stroll/Retna Ltd.; 72. Getty Images/Ron Galella/Wireimage; 73. Getty Images/Dave Hogan; 74. Getty Images/Luke Frazza/AFP; 75. Corbis/Chris Good/Retna Ltd.; 76. Getty Images/Laison; 77. Corbis/Greg Allen/Retna Ltd.; 78. Getty Images/Jean-Marc Giboux/Liasion; 79. Getty Images/Princess Diana Archive; 80. Retna; 82. Kobal Collection/Lucasfilm/Disney (top); 82. Mirrorpix (bottom); 84-85. Press Association Images/C.F. Tham; 86. Corbis/Diego Goldberg/Sygma; 87. Allstar Picture Library; 89. Getty Images/Phil Dent/Redferns; 90. Rex Features/HBO/Everett; 91. Getty Images/David McGough/DMI/Time & Life Pictures; 92. Corbis/Eric Robert/Sygma; 93. Press Association Images/Tsugufumi Matsumoto/AP; 94. Corbis/Reuters/Stringer (top); 94. Rex Features/Richard Young (bottom); 95. Rex Features; 96. Allstar Picture Library (top); 96. Corbis/Reuters/Stringer (bottom); 97. Corbis/Lynn Goldsmith; 99. Corbis/Mark Cardwell/Reuters; 100. Reuters; 102. Reuters; 103. Corbis/Patrick Robert/Sygma; 104. Rex Features/Sipa Press; 107. Allstar Picture Library; 108. Getty Images/Kevin Mazur/Wireimage; 109. Rex Features/Richard Young (top); 109. Rex Features/Sipa Press (bottom); 110-111. Getty Images/Steven Paul Whitsitt/Contourphotos.com; 112. www.splashnewsonline.com; 113. Corbis/Gary Hershorn/Reuters; 114-115. Getty Images/Dave Hogan; 117. Corbis/MR Photo/Outline; 118. Getty Images/Kevin Mazur/Wireimage (top); 118. Getty Images/AFP (bottom); 119. Corbis/Connie Aramaki/Epa; 120. Rex Features/Will Schneider (top); 120. Rex Features/KPA/Zuma (bottom); 121. Corbis/Reuters; 122. Getty Images/Kevin Kane/Wireimage (top); 122. www.bigpictures.co.uk (bottom); 123. Getty Images/Ian Barkley; 124-125. Corbis/MR Photo/Outline; 127. Getty Images/Kevin Mazur/AEG; 128. Getty Images/AFP; 128-129. Getty Images/Kevin Mazur/AEG; 131. Rex Features/KPA/Zuma; 132. Getty Images/Julien Hekimian/Wireimage; 133. Getty Images/Joshua Lott/Reuters (top); 133. Getty Images/Mark Ralston/AFP (bottom); 134. Getty Images/China Photos (top); 134. Corbis/Gene Blevins/LA Daily News (bottom); 135. Corbis/Retna Ltd.; 136-137. Press Association Images; 139. Rex Features; 140-141. Corbis/Mark Blinch/Reuters; 144. Getty Images/Al Messerschmidt

Every effort has been made to acknowledge correctly and contact the source and/or copyright holder of each picture, and Carlton Books apologizes for any unintentional errors or omissions, which will be corrected in future editions of this book.